FOLLOW HIM

AND RECLAIM THE WORLD

I0080612

Dennis J. Billy, CSsR

Liguori

Imprimi Potest:
Stephen T. Rehrauer, CSsR, Provincial
Denver Province, the Redemptorists

Published by Liguori Publications
Liguori, Missouri 63057

To order, visit Liguori.org or call 800-325-9521.

Library of Congress Cataloging-in-Publication Data
Billy, Dennis Joseph, author.
  Follow him : called to redeem the world / Fr. Dennis J. Billy, CSsR. — First edition.
     pages cm
  Includes bibliographical references.
  ISBN 978-0-7648-2650-4
  1. Jesus Christ—Person and offices. 2. Catholic Church—Doctrines. I. Title.
  BT203.B5354 2015
  232—dc23
                    2015030927

p ISBN 978-0-7648-2650-4
e ISBN 978-0-7648-7082-8

Liguori Publications, a nonprofit corporation, is an apostolate of the Redemptorists. To learn more about the Redemptorists, visit Redemptorists.com.

Printed in the United States of America
20 19 18 17 16 / 5 4 3 2 1
First Edition

In memory of

REV. ROBERT I. GANNON

1935–2008

In memory of

REV. ROBERT I. GANNON

1935–2008

Have among yourselves the same attitude that is also yours in Christ Jesus, Who, though he was in the form of God, did not regard equality with God something to be grasped. Rather, he emptied himself, taking the form of a slave, coming in human likeness; and found human in appearance, he humbled himself, becoming obedient to death, even death on a cross. Because of this, God greatly exalted him and bestowed on him the name that is above every name, that at the name of Jesus every knee should bend, of those in heaven and on earth and under the earth, and every tongue confess that Jesus Christ is Lord, to the glory of God the Father.

Philippians 2:5–11

Contents

Foreword

While this book is not about St. Alphonsus de Liguori (1696–1787) and rarely quotes him, it was definitely inspired by him. Being a member of the Redemptorist Congregation, the religious order he founded in 1732, I have been fascinated by the Gospel spirituality he preached to the neglected peasants in the small mountain hilltops and country villages of Southern Italy for many years and wondered how the basic ingredients of that message could be presented to the twenty-first-century reader. Aware of the perennial debate about whether there was only one Christian spirituality or many,[1] I also wondered how his preaching encapsulated the essence of the Gospel message and whether there was an underlying message that would be valid for all times, all places, and all circumstances.

My thoughts led me back to the Gospels themselves and the core narrative behind them: "God entered our broken world, gave himself completely to the point of dying for us, to become our nourishment and source of hope."[2] As I pondered this narrative, I gradually came to see that it corresponded perfectly with the four words that best summarize the essence of Alphonsian spirituality: crib, cross, sacrament, and Mary. Each word covers a different facet of this core Gospel narrative. "God entered our broken world" embraces the mystery of the Incarnation, which Alphonsus described with the word *crib*. "He gave himself completely to the point of dying for us" reveals the mystery of the passion, which Alphonsus summarized with the word *cross*. "He became nourishment for us" brings into focus the mystery of the Eucharist, which Alphonsus depicted with the word *sacrament*. "He became our source of hope" highlights the mystery of the resurrection and our hope of one day sharing fully in it, which Alphonsus aptly associates with Mary.

Crib. Cross. Sacrament. Mary.

Alphonsian spirituality embraces the essence of the Gospel message, for it treats each of its major mysteries: the Incarnation, the passion, the Eucharist, and our hope of one day experiencing—like Mary—the fullness of the Redemption. This authentic Gospel spirituality is the subject of this book. It is the core spirituality that inspired Alphonsus in his day, has inflamed countless others both before and after him and should continue to inspire Jesus' followers today, regardless of where they come from and how they understand their place in Christ's mystical body. This book is about the basics of Gospel spirituality; nothing more and nothing less. May the pages that follow inspire you, like St. Alphonsus, to make this Gospel narrative your own. May it challenge you to open your heart, think new thoughts, and find new ways of proclaiming the Good News of plentiful redemption.

Fr. Dennis J. Billy, CSsR
August 1, 2015
Feast of St. Alphonsus de Liguori

Introduction

> Then Jesus said to his disciples, "Whoever wishes to come after me must deny himself, take up his cross, and follow me. For whoever wishes to save his life will lose it, but whoever loses his life for my sake will find it. What profit would there be for one to gain the whole world and forfeit his life? Or what can one give in exchange for his life?
>
> *Matthew 16:24–26*

"Christianity," it has been said, "has not been tried and found wanting; it has been found difficult and not tried."[3] These words of G. K. Chesterton (1874–1936) highlight one of the current enigmas of the Christian story. What passes for Christianity today is often a watered-down version of what it really means to follow Jesus. In many areas of our contemporary lives, the cross has given way to a love for cultural accommodation and moral compromise that seriously threatens the authentic following of Christ. "The blood of the martyrs," which Tertullian (*circa* 160–*circa* 225) wrote was "the seed of the Church,"[4] seems to have been displaced by an exaggerated concern for self-fulfillment and the nonstop pursuit of the 3P's: pleasure, possessions, and power. This search has confused our consciences and made many indifferent to true Gospel values. We have forgotten the rigors that following Christ entails. Rather than a radical change in our outlook on life and the way we live it, Christianity becomes a nominal membership in just one of many clubs to which we belong and give our lukewarm allegiance.

This book seeks to take a deeper look at our faith by viewing it through the eyes of its founder, Jesus of Nazareth. This may be uncomfortable or seem like a tall order, especially since Christ died more than 2,000 years ago. Understanding his outlook and adapting it to our world today is a difficult but not impossible task to achieve. Our Christian story is based on the conviction that the Jesus of Nazareth who was crucified on Calvary rose from the dead and returned to his Father's right hand in a glorified state. The Jesus of history is one with the Christ of faith, and those who experienced him both historically and in his glorified state have left in the words of sacred Scripture an authentic testimony of his Spirit. What is more, this story asserts that we not only possess a fairly reliable record of Jesus' words and actions but also can live in his friendship and experience through his spirit an intimate communion of mind and heart.

The Apostle Paul makes the astounding claim to have the mind of Christ himself (1 Corinthians 2:16) and that this same Christ was alive and living within him (Galatians 2:20). We might say Jesus wishes to take possession of our hearts. He does so by renewing our minds and clothing us with a new self (Ephesians 4:24). For this to happen, two things in particular must enter our lives: the cross and the empty tomb. These symbols define the faith and make it possible for us to be real disciples of Christ. Christianity cannot exist without them, for they are both intimately tied to the passion, death, and resurrection of Christ himself. True and authentic followers of Christ allow these symbols to shape their lives and mold their outlook. To follow

Jesus means to embrace these symbols by living for others in love and expectant hope.

The book is based on a simple premise: To understand what it means to follow in the footsteps of Christ today we must first understand why he had footsteps in the first place. We must understand why God decided to visit this world in the person of Jesus Christ and what he did for the world through him.

For this to happen we need an adequate assessment of the world in all its created wonder and human brokenness. Then we must look at what God decided to do to heal the world and make it whole. The Christian story is based on the notion that our world has somehow gone awry and that God has decided to make things right by entering it and fixing it from the inside out. We believe that, in order to redeem our fallen world, God entered it by becoming flesh in the person of Jesus, who gave himself completely to the point of dying for us so that he could become our food, nourishment, and source of hope.

More importantly, by entering our world and setting it aright, God decided to elevate it to greater heights than ever. As far as humanity is concerned, he decided not merely to restore us to our former glory but to divinize us and bestow on us the possibility of becoming his adopted sons and daughters. This is the heritage of our Christian faith. To call ourselves Christian, we must espouse these fundamental values that are rooted in the life, death, and resurrection person of Jesus of Nazareth.

The book comprises five closely related chapters:

- **Chapter one, "Our Broken World,"** examines the Christian doctrines of creation and the Fall. It affirms the goodness of creation, the mystery of evil and sin, and the consequences of humanity's fall from grace.

13

- **Chapter two, "He Entered Our World,"** looks at the mystery of the Incarnation, focusing on the humility of God, who emptied himself to become one of us in order to heal and save us.

- **Chapter three, "He Gave of Himself Completely,"** focuses on the ministry, life, and death of Jesus. It depicts him as a man who lived entirely for others and who showed us the depths of his love by paying the ultimate price of death on the cross.

- **Chapter four, "He Became Our Nourishment,"** presents the Eucharist as the means by which Jesus makes his paschal mystery a reality in our daily lives. Through this sacrament, he gives us food for our spiritual journey, immerses us in the narrative of his passion, and makes himself present to us in a real and glorious way.

- **Chapter five, "He Became Our Source of Hope,"** shows how Jesus' resurrection offers hope for all humanity and points to the realization of our deepest dreams and longings.

Taken together, these chapters present the most basic truths of our Christian faith and lie at the heart of the call to discipleship. To help us delve more deeply into these mysteries, each chapter includes an unfolding, chapter-by-chapter story about God's presence in the lives of two troubled and searching hearts, a series of reflection questions encouraging us to engage the basic truths of the faith in a more personal manner, and a prayer to God asking for help in placing Christ at the center of our lives. The closing epilogue suggests what these mysteries might mean for the life of discipleship today.

An old saying addresses our present situation today very well: "If you were on trial for being a Christian, would there be enough evidence to convict you?" How would *you* answer this question? What evidence of deep Christian faith do you exhibit in your life? What witness do you give to Christ through your thoughts, words, and actions? How do you manifest God's love in your life? For many of us, the quest for holiness has been permanently placed on the back burner. Few of us take to heart the Second Vatican Council's emphasis on the universal call to holiness and how it lies at the heart of discipleship.[5] Instead, we have given in to the allure of the consumer and entertainment culture that characterizes so much of modern Western society and go through life numbed by our own complacency.

What does it mean to follow Christ in a world set adrift amidst the changing currents of individualism and relativism? How do we overcome our self-centeredness and human frailties? How do we focus on the one thing that matters? The challenges are daunting and the forces we struggle against seem overwhelming.

Is there enough evidence to convict YOU of being a Christian?

This book brings out the authentic dimensions of Christian discipleship. It reminds us that Jesus' story is also our story and that, like him, we're also called to enter the world of those around us and give ourselves to them completely as nourishment and a source of hope. The adventure of Christian discipleship is all about Jesus walking with us on our journey through life. It is about our lives being inextricably bound up with his. It is a constant reminder that the crosses we carry pale in comparison with the joy and hope that has been revealed to us as a result of the empty tomb. It empowers us to engage the world in constructive ways because we, like Jesus, are in it but not of it. It affirms the power of hope over despair, of love over hatred, of life over death. It believes there is nothing to be afraid of because the Lord has overcome the powers of darkness, and his kingdom of light is near at hand.

Chapter One

Our Broken World

This is the story of the heavens and the earth at their creation. When the LORD God made the earth and the heavens—there was no field shrub on earth and no grass of the field had sprouted, for the LORD God had sent no rain upon the earth and there was no man to till the ground, but a stream was welling up out of the earth and watering all the surface of the ground—then the LORD God formed the man out of the dust of the ground and blew into his nostrils the breath of life, and the man became a living being.

The LORD God planted a garden in Eden, in the east, and placed there the man whom he had formed. Out of the ground the LORD God made grow every tree that was delightful to look at and good for food, with the tree of life in the middle of the garden and the tree of the knowledge of good and evil.

Genesis 2:4–9

Key Themes

- Original sin is responsible for our belief in creation's inherent limitations.
- God created the world with a fundamental goodness.
- After the Fall we are left with a bleeding vulnerability and hidden hope for redemption.

Questions about the nature of the world—its origin, makeup, scope, and destiny—have captivated curious minds for all time. Primitive peoples resorted to myth to explain the cosmos and their place in it. Philosophers have used reason to unravel its meaning. Scientists have drawn conclusions about the universe from experiments rooted in empirical observation. Adherents of the world's major religions have relied on faith to fathom its depths and unlock its mysteries.

We have something in common with each of these approaches. We believe the Christian story of Jesus' passion, death, and resurrection is "myth become fact."[6] Having certain basic presuppositions about the relationship between faith and reason, we have drawn some concrete conclusions about the world and humanity's place in it. We have a particular outlook toward the world that is rooted in reason, enhanced by revelation, and increasingly at odds with the values of the present age.

Creation and Fall

Our Christian worldview has its roots in the stories of creation and the Fall. The opening chapters of Genesis actually contain two accounts of creation: one where God makes man and woman on the sixth day before his Sabbath rest (Genesis 1—2:4) and the other where their creation occurs respectively before and after the creation of the Garden of Eden (Genesis 2:5–25). These two stories complement each other in a way that highlights some of the basic truths of Christian anthropology.

The first account puts humanity at the summit of God's creation, placing us in a position of responsible dominion and lordship over the rest of creation. The second emphasizes that Eden was created for us and that we have been given the responsibility to cultivate and care for it. Each account draws a close link between humanity and the world as manifestations of God's creative power through several key points:

- Each places us in a position of authority over the rest of creation.

- Each highlights our noble origins by stating that God created man and woman in his image and likeness (Genesis 1—2:4) and by presenting man as a living being when God breathes into his nostrils (Genesis 2:5–25).

- Each points to the complementary aspects of the relationship between man and woman: the first, by stressing their fundamental dignity by virtue of their being created in God's image and likeness (Genesis 1:27); the second, by accentuating their complementary nature with God, giving man a companion who is bone from his bones and flesh from his flesh (Genesis 2:23).

Follow Him

Taken together, these accounts emphasize the goodness of creation, our basic human dignity, and the harmony of our relationships with God, each other, and all creation. They make major contributions to the Christian worldview and form the backdrop of the drama of creation, sin, and redemption that lies at the heart of the Gospel message.

The stories of the Fall (Genesis 3) and the subsequent downward spiral of hatred and violence that has plagued us since the dawn of time (Genesis 4—11) introduce another important element into the mix: the presence of evil. These accounts counter the paradisal view of the creation stories with the story of humanity's fall from grace. According to this view, evil enters the world through the cunning of a snake, a creature generally associated with Satan and the powers of darkness. Adam and Eve converse with this evil creature and disobey God's command against eating the fruit of the tree of knowledge of good and evil, thinking the action will make them "be like gods" (Genesis 3:5). As a result, humanity senses its nakedness, tries to hide its shame, and is cast out of Eden once God surmises what it has done.

Because of our sin, our willful "missing the mark" or falling out of step with God, we suffer from physical hardships, death, and broken, dysfunctional relationships for the rest of our earthy sojourn. The accounts in Genesis that follow—those of Cain and Abel (Genesis 4:1–16), the patriarchs before the Flood, (Genesis 5:1–32), Noah and the Flood (Genesis 6:5—9:28), the Tower of Babel (Genesis 11:1–9) the patriarchs after the Flood (Genesis 11:10–26), the destruction of Sodom and Gomorrah (Genesis 19:1–29)—chart the violent downward spiral of hatred, violence, sin, and destruction that we struggle with to this day.

These stories of creation and the Fall tell us that, while sin entered the world through our cooperation with the powers of darkness, evil obscures but does not completely overcome the fundamental goodness of God's creation. In exchange for the knowledge of good and evil, we have lost our intimate relationship with God, creation, and ourselves and replaced it with a life of toil, hardship, and endless struggle.

From these realities, Augustine of Hippo (354–430) developed his doctrine of original sin, which described Adam's Fall as a sin of pride affecting all human nature, passing from one generation to the next through sexual intercourse, resulting in a cataclysmic fall from grace and making human beings incapable of meritorious action.[7] A few centuries earlier, Irenaeus of Lyons (*circa* 180) interpreted the Fall as the stumbling first steps of an infant humanity, an event that would pale in comparison with all things that would eventually be wrought by Christ's divinizing transformation of humanity.[8] Under either interpretation, our fall from grace results in our living with deep wounds in a broken world that, except for some dramatic divine intervention, would make us incapable of virtuous living, let alone an elevation to heights never before imagined. Today the Church teaches that the account of the Fall "uses figurative language, but affirms a primeval event, a deed that took place at the beginning of the history of man." "Revelation," it goes on to say, "gives us the certainty of faith that the whole of human history is marked by the original fault freely committed by our first parents."[9]

Our Christian Worldview

Together these creation stories affirm the goodness of creation, the presence of evil in the world, the reality of sin (original, personal, or otherwise), and our need for redemption. They set the stage for the drama of Christ's Incarnation, passion, death, resurrection, and ascension into heaven. These Christian doctrines only make sense because the world we live in is finite and in drastic need of repair. God believed in humanity even when humanity had lost faith in itself, and our Christian story affirms that. It says that God dramatically intervened in the world to save us from ourselves.

All mature theological reflection involves the interplay of three key concepts: God, humanity, and the world.[10] We are not isolated actors on the world stage but intimately bound up with the world around us. We are a part of the world, and our actions affect it for better or for worse. Our destiny and that of the world are closely intertwined. Where we go the world goes—and vice versa. What takes place within our human souls has repercussions far beyond its borders. Our good actions have a positive effect on the world; our sinful actions are detrimental to it. We can work to preserve the world or pollute it; tend it or tear it down; be its caretakers or its undertakers. The choice was, is, and will be ours to make.

Our actions affect not only the world around us but also our own selves. Every human action, every deliberated action of reason and will, has consequences both for us and our world. It also matters to God. When seen in this light, the sin of Adam has serious ramifications for the human heart and the entire cosmos. Because humanity is intimately tied up with the world, the sin of human origins is also the sin of the world's origins. At some point in our collective existence, we decided to turn from God and go our own way. The biblical accounts of sin spiral from the pride of Adam, to the fratricide of Cain, to the ruins of Babel, to the decadence of Sodom and Gomorrah, and continue to this day. We acknowledge that something has gone terribly wrong in the world and that we, by choosing to follow our own will, have somehow caused it, become victims of it, and cannot make it right on our own. We place our hope not in humanity, but in the intervention of divine love in human affairs. This Christian view of the world centers on a loving and compassionate God who creates, redeems, and sanctifies. We hope in a God who promises to make all things new by transforming the old order and carrying it to the threshold of the divine.

Real-World View: A Story of Faith

The wise have eyes in their head,
but fools walk in darkness.

Ecclesiastes 2:14

Dorothy is a single, middle-aged woman with a deep wound in her heart. She got pregnant when she was a senior in high school and her boyfriend pressured her into having an abortion. She felt the abortion was wrong, but agreed with her boyfriend's argument that they were too young. They had their whole lives ahead of them. A child would limit them. They'd be trapped with no real way to provide for the baby. They weren't prepared for this.

She thought about having the child and putting him up for adoption, but she was scared of telling her parents about the pregnancy. *What would they think of her? How would they react? What would they say?* So she and her boyfriend kept the pregnancy a secret. She had the abortion at an out-of-town clinic so as few people as possible would know.

She knew about it, though. And she carried that guilt deep in her heart ever since. Dorothy and her boyfriend broke up about a year later and she lost touch as he moved on to build a life with someone else. She has carried the guilt of ending the pregnancy around with her for a long time, and it has made her very unhappy, even angry—at her boyfriend, her family, at the world, and especially at herself. She feels broken inside and doesn't know what to do about it. She's afraid to enter into another romantic relationship because she doesn't want to let anyone that close again. She doesn't want to be let down again.

She feels estranged from God and has even convinced herself he doesn't exist. Deep down she knows she's rationalizing his existence away, just as she rationalized away the death of her child. She puts up a good front, but inside it feels as though she is a broken woman living in a broken world. She was raised in a devout Catholic family but tells herself that she has outgrown the faith of her childhood. She has convinced her mind; now if only she could convince her heart.

Her life has turned out very different from the way she thought it would. She has buried herself in her work, has few friends, and feels burdened by the secret she has been carrying all these years. She needs to tell someone but is afraid of trying. She doesn't even know where to begin. She escapes from her guilt by self-medicating with alcohol and prescription drugs.

One year at the office Christmas party she had one too many. That was the day Jim entered her life.

Reflect

- How would you describe Dorothy's world?

- Where does her pain come from?

- Have you ever felt the way she does? What are positive ways to deal with this kind of pain?

Taking a Deeper Look: Sin

By looking closer at sin and its consequences, we see the Fall as a more complex event than just two people not following a rule. Through this deeper understanding we see how sin and the Fall touched God, humanity, and the world as well as why we needed redemption and still suffer and sin today.

Our fall from grace has disrupted our friendship with God.

That God would create us in his image and likeness implies that he has a unique fondness for us and our ancestors. Rather than projecting human qualities onto God, when we study human nature we see the reflection of God himself. We were created to be an icon of the divine which, when prayerfully contemplated, would reveal something of God's mystery and majesty to the world. By studying the noblest qualities of our nature, we can assume that God is spiritual, social, rational, willful, virtuous, loving, and capable of intimate friendship. We could also conclude that God created us in his image and likeness so that he could enter into relationship with us and with all creation. Original sin not only tarnished God's image and likeness in us but also broke the bonds of friendship God had forged with us. Rather than communing with God, we were set on a course of increasing isolation. This spilled over into all our other relationships and turned what was meant to be a garden paradise into what many deemed a living hell.

Our fall from grace has also had repercussions for all creation.

Evil already existed in the spiritual realm of the demonic powers, but when it crept into our human hearts it wreaked havoc not only in our inner world but also in the visible world we inhabited. Our fall from grace had a ripple effect on the entire universe. When Adam sinned, the whole created order fell with him. The goodness of creation, while never completely compromised, became tarnished and bent out of shape. All creation shared in our rebellion against the created order of things and became a willful, if unwitting, accomplice to our sinfulness. When the harmonious order of creation was broken in our failed attempt to usurp the role of the divine, the resulting disorder in our hearts filtered down to all other levels of the visible world. "Everything is connected," the saying goes. After the Fall, all that was left in our memory was a vague recollection that paradise was lost and that we had played a decisive role in losing it.

Our fall from grace has wounded, not completely destroyed, our human nature.

Experience tells us that despite our vast shortcomings we remain essentially good. Our wounds can be healed and we can be made whole, just not on our own. As with the rest of creation, human nature is not evil or totally corrupted. We are fundamentally good. We are still created in the image and likeness of God, even though that image has been tarnished by sin. Original sin means that we have collectively fallen short of the mark laid out for us by God. These shortcomings have taken root deep in our unconscious and filled us with fear and anxiety, but we can be redeemed, and redemption is our deepest longing and enduring hope.

Our fall from grace has heightened our experience of suffering.

This shift in our nature also brought changes in our awareness of pain and our interpretation of its meaning. What was formerly understood as an integral and necessary part of life was now perceived as an existential threat to be avoided at all costs. Suffering became valueless and meaningless. It was thought to penetrate every aspect of human experience—the physical, the emotional, the intellectual, the social, and even the spiritual—and was viewed as part of the daily, inescapable drudgery of human existence. Suffering was often seen as a result of being out of communion with God. Suffering was even inflicted on others to bend their wills and used as a threat to force others to conform to the designs of the powerful. We came to believe there was no escape and that suffering on earth was nothing but a harbinger of the ultimate suffering of the separation of body and soul at death.

Our fall from grace has made us fearful of death and traumatized us about the end of life.

It is commonly thought that death entered the world as a result of Adam's sin. While this may well be true, it is also possible that it was the *fear* of death, and the hidden suspicion that it marked the end of our existence, that traumatized us after our fall from grace. Prior to that time, death was viewed merely as a natural stage of life that would lead to a higher form of existence; however, as our relationship with God became severely damaged it led to a fundamental distrust of the natural course of things. As a result, death was perceived as a great upheaval within the person. Rather than leading us to a higher state of life, the separation of the body from the soul signaled a lonely end to a doomed existence.

Our fall from grace has led
to a weakening of our capacity to reason.

Before the Fall, we shared an intimate fellowship with God. One sign of this fellowship was our capacity to think with God and anticipate his action in our lives. This deep sharing in his life meant that we were able to think clearly about our relationship to him, the ties we share with each other, and our place in the universe. After the Fall, this intimate fellowship with God was deeply marred. Our reasoning power shrank to a mere shadow of its former self. Our intuitive knowledge of what was right and wrong was gravely damaged. The once blazing fire within our hearts dwindled to a mere spark, and this tiny spark of conscience could be covered by the darkness of sin. Truth itself began to be perceived as fragmented and split apart. We began wondering if reason itself was nothing more than a thin veneer that disguised irrational appetites. Even when we *did* exalt reason during the course of history, we could never recover our intimate participation in the wisdom of God we had lost at the dawn of our existence.

Our fall from grace has weakened
our ability to will the good.

Before the Fall, we walked in fellowship with God, sharing the same intention and desire: to do his will. As a result of the Fall, we experienced a weakening not only of our reasoning powers but also of the command of our will and our ability to freely choose what is good. Our will became vulnerable to internal and external forces that we previously could control. This loss of sovereignty resulted in our enslavement to all kinds of temptations, false dreams, illusory pleasures, and addictions. With our power to choose seriously damaged, we lost our capacity to make and implement sound judgments. The virtuous life became an elusive, unrealizable goal, while vices overpowered us. Deep in our hearts, we knew what was right but could not follow it. We gave in easily to the allures of the flesh, the praise of men, and the temptations to honor and glory. We could not resist the enticements of the evil one, let alone our own reasoning, which led us off the path of holiness.

Our fall from grace has disordered our feelings and emotions, making them wild and unruly.

Before the Fall, our emotions were ruled by rational powers. After the Fall, we rebelled against these rational powers and carved out our own path. The result was that we became increasingly ruled by our animal passions, and the capital sins of lust, gluttony, greed, sloth, wrath, envy, and pride gained sway over our minds. This topsy-turvy arrangement in which passions trumped reason and will cast human society into a cloud of darkness from which it could not escape. The animal side took precedence over the spiritual, and our rational side became increasingly subject to the whims of desire.

Our fall from grace has affected our social well-being.

Human beings are social creatures by nature, as we see in the centrality of the family in society, the tendency we have to associate in groups according to common interests, or to form governments and nation-states for our economic and societal welfare. Before the Fall, our familial and societal relationships reflected the harmony of our relationships with God and the rest of creation. Although those relationships may have been relatively simple (even primitive) by today's standards, they nonetheless show an ideal unity of spirit that allowed for our development and growth in an environment free of dysfunction. After the Fall, our wounded nature affected our ability to form and sustain these ideal social relationships. Sound human relationships became increasingly difficult and, in some cases, impossible to form. The never-ending stream of abuse, crime, and violence that has haunted us throughout history has become commonplace in today's world. Having lost faith in our neighbors, we approached each other with mistrust and a deep, recognizable fear of being taken advantage of.

The final result of our fall from grace has been a withering of our human spirit.

Before the Fall, the human spirit was a vital part of everyday life and integrated with every other dimension of human existence. After the Fall, it became withered and dry, isolated from the divine, from other human beings, as well as from the other aspects of our individual makeup. The result was a loss of fellowship with God and others that manifested itself as an empty hole and a deep inner loneliness in our hearts. From then on, we would spend most of our energy trying to fill that emptiness with all sorts of created goods and pleasures, only to come up short. Nothing could satisfy the emptiness we experienced. Having forsaken the infinite for the finite, we failed to recognize the shortcomings of the created order and forgot that it was made for God and nothing or no one else.

Although our human spirit was withered, it was not dead. We needed to be resuscitated and refreshed by life-giving waters that would enable us to once again commune with the divine and live in fellowship with our maker.

Conclusion

The Gospel message views the world as a creation of a loving God who shaped humanity, the summit of his creation, in his own image and likeness. It asserts that we play an integral role in the maintenance, care, and future development of the world. It also holds that the world's destiny and our own are deeply intertwined. Through its doctrine of the Fall, Christianity maintains that our turning from God at the dawn of time had repercussions on the whole of creation. The rebellion that went on deep within our hearts spilled over into the cosmos.

We see faith and reason as complementary spheres of knowledge about reality: the insights of the first are rooted in revelation; those of the second, in reason. Because of the Fall, our powers of reason and will were seriously weakened, affecting our capacity to make sound judgments and unbiased observations. Our weakened nature has led us along a downward spiral of self-centeredness and increasing isolation. Our broken nature is in desperate need of repair and is itself both a cause and a symptom of the damaged world it inhabits.

As followers of Christ, we view the whole of creation as seriously flawed and desperately in need of redemption. We believe that Jesus Christ became one of us to remedy the world's ills, and that he is its one and only Savior. We maintain that only an act of infinite love could turn back the tide of rebellion that began in the heart of humanity's first parents and has reverberated throughout the entire universe to this day. We envision not merely a creation restored to its original beauty but a *new* creation thoroughly transformed and elevated to heights never before imagined.

We see this new creation up close in the mystery of the Incarnation. Jesus Christ is the new Adam, whose humanity reflects not merely the image and likeness of God but has itself become thoroughly divinized. We affirm that our humanity is now intimately tied to his and that creation itself has been blessed with a heavenly destiny.

Deepening Our Awareness

- What do you believe about the world you inhabit? Is it finite or eternal, good or evil, unfinished, a work in progress, broken beyond repair, deserving of salvation, chaotic or created?

- Is your view of the world similar to Dorothy's? Why or why not?

- Where do your beliefs about the world come from: home, religion, peers, education, or other areas?

- What role has society played in your views about the world and your place in it?

- Do you continuously evaluate your beliefs either in your own mind or in conversations with others?

- Do your beliefs change often or are you rigid in them? Do they hold a place in both your head and your heart? What would your life be like without them?

- What about the Christian worldview do you find attractive? What do you find difficult to accept?

A Disciple's Prayer

Lord, I look around me and see that I live in a broken world desperately in need of healing. I find this brokenness all around me, even deep within my heart. There is so much trouble and unrest. Violence and hatred abound. Ethnic and racial tensions have boiled over. Nations are at war. Religious unrest runs rampant. Freedom has given way to addiction. All of creation seems infected with a deadly contagion. Sometimes it seems as though the world will not make it through another day. Sometimes I even feel the same about myself. Everything around me seems to be unraveling. In the midst of my brokenness, I cry out to you and turn to you as my Creator and Lord. You hold the world in existence and have blessed it with a deep-down goodness that no wound can ever completely erase. I refuse to lose hope. I will not allow darkness to overwhelm me. I turn to you because you are not only the world's creator but also its Savior. Help me to welcome you into the world this day. Help me to join you in your loving embrace. Help me to find you in the deepest crevices of my heart and the darkest moments of my world. Amen.

Chapter Two

He Entered Our World

In the beginning was the Word, and the Word was with God, and the Word was God. He was in the beginning with God. All things came to be through him, and without him nothing came to be. What came to be through him was life, and this life was the light of the human race; the light shines in the darkness, and the darkness has not overcome it. A man named John was sent from God. He came for testimony, to testify to the light, so that all might believe through him. He was not the light, but came to testify to the light. The true light, which enlightens everyone, was coming into the world. He was in the world, and the world came to be through him, but the world did not know him. He came to what was his own, but his own people did not accept him. But to those who did accept him he gave power to become children of God, to those who believe in his name, who were born not by natural generation nor by human choice nor by a man's decision but of God. And the Word became flesh and made his dwelling full of grace and truth.

John 1:1–14

Key Themes

- The impact of God's incarnate love reverberates throughout the entire cosmos and has a lasting effect.

- God empowers us to be stewards of creation in a way never before possible.

- A divinized humanity works from within to create the world anew and make it a fitting place for the incarnate God of love to inhabit.

As a result of the Fall, we lived in a broken world and were paralyzed by sin and self-centeredness. We had departed from God's plan and were destined to wander aimlessly through history without purpose or direction. Having forsaken God, we became lost and had no way of finding him. Only God could set things right, and that is precisely what he chose to do. Our Christian story is not about how we find the way to heaven but about God finding his way to us.

The Old Testament sketches the history of God's revelation to his people as they struggled to find their bearings in a fallen world. It follows the history of the Jewish people and tells of a series of covenants God made with his chosen ones at various points in history—with Noah (Genesis 6:18; 9:8-17), Abraham (Genesis 15:1-21), Moses and the people of Israel (Exodus 20:22—23:19; Deuteronomy 4:44—26:19); David and his lineage (1 Samuel 16:1-13; 2 Samuel 5:1-3; 2 Samuel 7:1-17). Those culminated in the promise to the prophet Jeremiah that a New Covenant with his people would come (Jeremiah 31:31-34).[11] This New Covenant has been extended to all people and was established by the coming of God as man in the person of Jesus Christ.

"The Word Became Flesh"

God's response to our broken world was to create it anew from the inside out. To do this, he entered our world and became one with his creation in a way that went far beyond his original creative act in Genesis. God would become one with us by uniting himself to us through the mystery of the Incarnation.

Saint Athanasius of Alexandria (295–373) once said that God became human so humanity might become divine.[12] The mystery of the Incarnation did not erase the distinction between us and God, but through it God heals our wounds and transforms us. Some people think this mystery of the Incarnation stretches the limits of imagination. But this is precisely the sort of thing that an all-loving, all-knowing, and all-powerful God would do! Our God is a God of surprises. He calls us out of our humdrum ways of viewing things and challenges us to get in touch with our deepest longings. Why would God become man? Well, why wouldn't he? Why wouldn't the mystery of love express itself in this seemingly impossible and thoroughly surprising way? Humanity, after all, is the summit of God's creation.

> **Why would God become man? Well, why wouldn't he?**

God entered our world by becoming flesh and dwelling among us (John 1:14). He took on our human nature while retaining his divinity. The Word of God (what the Greeks called *Logos* and the Jews referred to as *Sophia*, or Divine Wisdom) descended from eternity and entered the womb of a humble virgin, Mary of Nazareth. This woman had been especially prepared through the movement of divine grace to open her heart to the angel Gabriel's message, to conceive by the power of the Holy Spirit, and to bear a son who would be called Jesus, Son of the Most High (Luke 1:26–32). Her simple *fiat* to God's plan for her, and all humanity, meant that her child would be fathered by God himself and would be fully human and fully divine (Luke 1:38).

Even though Mary was troubled by the angel's message (Luke 1:26), she embraced God's will for her with an open heart and a willingness to do whatever was asked of her (Luke 1:26–38). Her Magnificat was a prayer of praise that exulted the greatness of God and the powerful way he had chosen to work through her and in all humanity (Luke 1:46–55). She prayed to God with joyous abandon, even though she knew that her own heart would be pierced by a sword of sorrow (Luke 2:35) and her Son would suffer a painful death. Mary is Mother of both joy and sorrow. She was the first to hear the Good News of God's plan and responded to that news by pondering the angel's message in her heart. She was also the first to share this Good News with others when she visited her pregnant cousin Elizabeth, and John leaped when Mary greeted his mother (Luke 1:39–56).

That leap in the darkness of the womb represents the beginning of John's vocation of heralding the coming of the Lord. He was the last of the Old Testament prophets and the first of the New. As the precursor of God's anointed one, he baptized with water but saw the coming of one mightier than he, one who would baptize with the Holy Spirit and fire (Luke 3:16).

"And Dwelled Among Us"

God's journey into human history took shape in Nazareth in Galilee at the moment of the annunciation (Luke 1:26–38). With this crucial piece in place, the mystery of the Incarnation continued to unfold, first with Mary's marriage to Joseph

(Matthew 1:18–25), then with birth of the Child Jesus in Bethlehem (Matthew 2:1), and followed by the Holy Family's flight to Egypt (Matthew 2:13–15), the slaughter of the innocents (Matthew 2:16–18), their eventual return from Egypt (Matthew 2:19–23), and Jesus' hidden life in Nazareth (Matthew 2:23).

Mary and Joseph were not welcomed when they traveled to Bethlehem to register for the Roman census. With no room in the inn, they found lodging in what was probably a cave used as a stable to protect the animals from the elements (Luke 2:1–13). In that dark womb of the earth, the Savior of the world came forth from the darkness, was wrapped in swaddling clothes, and laid in a manger. In this way, Jesus' paschal mystery was strangely foreshadowed at the moment of his birth. As the Christmas story unfolds, many other incidents foreshadow the events of his life:

- The cave pointed to the empty tomb.
- the swaddling clothes, to his burial cloths,
- the manger, to the table from which Christians would partake of his Body and Blood,
- the angel's announcement of his birth to the shepherds reflects his message of love to the poor and lowly,
- the journey of the Magi, to the impact of his message on the Gentile nations,
- the slaughter of the holy innocents, to his horrible death by crucifixion, and
- the Holy Family's flight to Egypt and eventual return point to humanity's ultimate liberation from the enslavement of sin and death.

The manner in which God entered our world says something about the humility of God himself. When becoming man, God did not assume privileged status but united himself with our struggles, being like us in all things but sin (Hebrews 4:15). Doing so was an expression of divine self-effacement in the light of a greater good: our salvation and the shaping of a new creation. The Apostle Paul describes this willful self-impoverishment: "Who, though he was in the form of God, did not regard equality with God something to be grasped. Rather, he emptied himself, taking the form of a slave, coming in human likeness; and found human in appearance" (Philippians 2:6–7). The Good News of Christianity is rooted in the mystery of a loving God willing to take extravagant steps to bring humanity back to him. The mystery of the Incarnation was not necessary for the world's redemption but was an entirely free and gratuitous expression of God's love for wayward humanity. "God," in the famous words of St. Alphonsus de Liguori, was *Il Dio pazzo*," a crazy God madly in love with humanity.[13]

Our Christian story is not about how we find the way to heaven but about God finding his way to us.

This mystery highlights the beginning of God's humble self-emptying. Jesus was not born into wealth and prosperity but to a family that struggled to make ends meet. Although he came from the royal line of David, that lineage had been obscured over time and meant little to the powers of the day. He was born into a nation where hope of a coming Messiah ran deep in people's veins. Mary and Joseph nurtured that hope in their newborn Son and pondered the mystery of his birth and its significance for the Jewish people deep in their hearts. They gave him a stable home, loving hearts, the faith of their ancestors, and a deep reverence for God. They also kept him hidden from those who might feel threatened by him. Little else is known about Jesus' early life in Nazareth. We can only surmise that he lived the normal life of a first-century Galilean Jew, one that centered on family and deep religious devotion.

What little we know of Jesus' hidden life comes from Luke's Gospel. There he is presented not as someone who has all the answers but someone willing and ready to learn with an open heart. Although he impresses those in the Temple with his intelligent responses, he is portrayed primarily as someone eager to learn and ask questions. Jesus' quest for wisdom involves pondering the depths of the law and the prophets in the light of his intimate relationship with the Father. He astounds the teachers of the law (and his parents) because he is learning how to listen to the promptings of the Holy Spirit in his heart. In doing so, he has tapped into the depths of divine wisdom. At the age of twelve, Jesus is fast approaching the maturity of insight that will mark his public ministry. The account of the finding in the Temple reminds us that Jesus' relationship with the Father was carefully nurtured throughout his early life. It reminds us that God not only entered our world but lived among us and advanced in wisdom and age before both God and man.

Real-World View: A Story of Faith

Healing the brokenhearted,
and binding up their wounds.

Psalm 147:3

Jim is single, a few years older than Dorothy, and works for the same company in an office just down the hall. He was at the Christmas party the night she passed out and took control of the situation when things got out of hand. He drove her to a nearby hospital to have her checked out. At the hospital they determined Dorothy had overdosed on painkillers and had to have her stomach pumped. Jim stayed the whole night beside her hospital bed.

When Dorothy opened her eyes the next morning, the first person she saw was Jim. She didn't recognize him at first; she didn't even know where she was. Jim asked her how she was feeling and, when she was ready, filled in the embarrassing details about what happened at the party the night before. He did this in a kind and gentle manner. He could sense that she had something else going on inside and needed someone to lean on during this difficult time. He helped her deal with the embarrassment by taking the focus off her and sharing some of the many times he had made a fool of himself by his own dumb choices.

He was able to make her laugh and shift the attention away from her. He confessed he had a drinking problem and how it was only through the intervention of some close friends that he was able to pick up the pieces of his fragmented life. He also told her that, after many years of counseling and Alcoholics Anonymous meetings, he had come to see he was using alcohol as a way of blotting out the painful memories of abuse at the hands of his alcoholic father. He drank to fill a void caused by the lack of love in his life and to ease the pain of feeling he was unworthy of love, that it was somehow all his fault. He told her he had come to see that drinking was his way of escaping the past, numbing the pain of the present, and not taking hold of the reins of his life. He told her that the reason he had never married was because he had become married to his addiction.

He also shared that he hadn't had a drink for more than ten years and they had been the best years of his life. Jim's moving story touched Dorothy deeply. It resonated in her and made her feel better. Dorothy didn't feel comfortable sharing her own troubles with him (at least, not yet) but sensed he was a kindred spirit and someone she would like to know better. She liked talking to him and began wondering if this was a man she could trust. She opened up to him in small ways and was amazed at how comfortable she felt. She had known him before as a familiar face, someone to say hello to in the morning and make small talk with, but she now felt there was something deeper there. They were slowly becoming friends.

She had never talked that way with anyone before, and she wondered if there was a deeper purpose in their meeting. Jim seemed to come out of nowhere. He entered her world one day, and her life didn't feel quite the same. She felt as though someone cared for her. Maybe she would be able to share her story with him. She wondered if he would listen.

If God existed, did he have a part in all of this?

Reflect

• •

- What similarities are there between the way Jim entered Dorothy's life and the mystery of the Incarnation? What is different?

- In what way does Jim represent Christ to Dorothy?

- Have you ever experienced the love of Christ through another person?

Taking a Deeper Look: Incarnation

The mystery of the Incarnation is about the wisdom of God himself entering our world, taking on our humanity, and living among us. It defies description because it involves the divine becoming human, the Word becoming flesh, the infinite embracing the finite. Here's a deeper look at this mystery.

Incarnation involves a unique and unprecedented relationship between the human and the divine.

The Incarnation rests on the assumption that an all-powerful God is capable of entering creation and experiencing it through human eyes. The relationship between the human and divine in the person of Jesus is tied to the phrase *hypostatic union*. This traditional teaching affirms that Jesus was fully human and fully divine and that he was one and the same with the *Logos*, the second person of the Blessed Trinity. The nature of the relationship between the human and divine, while unique to the person of Jesus himself, also has repercussions for humanity and all creation. God became human so we could participate in his divinity. This means the world itself was also destined to be transformed and share in this process of divinization.

Incarnation, God's response to a world gone awry.

God created the world so we could enter into relationship with him. When we freely chose to leave that relationship, the choice had consequences for the rest of creation. The Incarnation is the divine response to humanity's fall from grace. God redeems both us and the world we live in by entering it, healing its wounds, and raising it to new heights.

Incarnation would have happened even if humanity had never fallen.

The transformation of humanity through Jesus was not necessarily tied to the Fall and could be seen as another stage in God's creative action. If Adam hadn't sinned, we would have walked in fellowship with God but wouldn't have received the gift of divine adoption. The Incarnation represents another stage in God's creative activity. It would have happened eventually. For this reason, the Incarnation can be called the beginning of a new creation. It orients us and the world we inhabit to a new destiny, one that lies in the heart of the Godhead itself.

Incarnation has repercussions for all of human history.

The impact of the Incarnation on human history becomes clear when we understand that time and space are created entities. By entering into this multidimensional world, God has brought his creation even further under the sway of his providential care. The incarnate Christ draws all of human history to himself. All events before and after his appearance on earth lead up to him and take their meaning from him. Salvation history is not separate from the flow of human events. It represents a special current within the general flow of history. The mystery of the Incarnation has radically shaped the course of world history and must lie at the heart of its movement, narrative, and purpose.

Incarnation has repercussions for our lives.

Christ gave each of us the opportunity to become sons and daughters of the Father. When we believe in him we become united with him, the story of his life becomes intimately bound up with ours—and vice versa. The mystery of the Incarnation weaves its way into the fabric of our souls. What took place in the heart of Mary also takes place in us. The Word of God, who is eternally begotten by the Father, conceived by the Holy Spirit, and born of the Virgin Mary, is being conceived by the Spirit to this day and born within the hearts and souls of all who believe.

Incarnation had an effect on God.

One of the classic problems of natural theology has to do with the impassibility of God. If change implies some element of imperfection, and if God is perfect, then how can God be said to change? But if he cannot change, how does he think and interact with his creation? The answers to these questions lie deep in the mystery of the Godhead and cannot be answered by our limited capacity for understanding. One way philosophers and theologians have tried to explain this mystery is juxtaposing the classical Greek concept of perfection (God does not change) with the classical Hebrew conception of God (God loves his people and intervenes in history) to present a conception of God that holds God's impassibility and his lordship of history in dynamic tension. In doing so, the mystery of the Godhead is preserved even more. God both changes and is changeless. The mystery of the Incarnation highlights this because it affirms that while the Father may remain impassible, his only-begotten Son walked this earth and experienced life and death in a way that touched the heart of divinity itself.

Incarnation has ramifications
for the way we read the Scriptures.

Christians believe that Jesus Christ represents the fullness of God's revelation to humanity. Because of this belief, all of Scripture can now be read in the light of Christ. Early on in their history, Christians began reading the Scriptures of the Jewish people in the light of Jesus' passion, death, and resurrection. To a large extent, the New Testament represents a collection of writings about Jesus as a representation of the fulfillment of the deepest hopes of Israel. While the Scriptures are a collection of disparate literary works written at various times and for different literary purposes, they hold together as a unified testament of God's dealings with his Chosen People and, because of the coming of Christ, all humanity. Because of the Incarnation, Scripture now reveals to us not merely knowledge about God, but the face of God himself. Through the action of the Holy Spirit, Scripture provides a place in which God speaks to the human heart and draws it to himself. Scripture, in other words, mediates the experience of the divine to us and fosters the birth of God's Word in our hearts.

Incarnation lies at the heart
of the Church's sacramental system.

If a sacrament is understood as a visible sign of invisible grace, then the whole economy of salvation can be described in this way:

- Christ is the sacrament of God.

- The Church is the sacrament of Christ.

- The seven sacraments are the sacraments of the Church.

Here the word *sacrament* has different shades of meaning, depending on what it's referring to. These differences are overcome in the mystery of the Incarnation, which lies at the heart of the sacramental system and brings the continuity of God's salvific action to each of these levels. Without the Incarnation and all that flows from it, there would not be a concrete, visible expression of our salvation. The Church would not be the manner through which he conveys his salvific grace throughout history. And the seven sacraments would not be considered the ordinary means of salvation. The Incarnation is the means ordained by God to mediate the saving mysteries of salvation to humanity.

Incarnation has important ramifications for Christian prayer.

By becoming man, God has established a divine-and-human mediator between heaven and earth. All Christian prayer is done through, with, and in our Lord Jesus Christ. Whenever we pray, we do so as members of Christ's mystical body, the Church. We approach the threshold of the divine not on our own but through the humanity of Christ, who intercedes for us. The theology of Christian prayer is rooted in the mystery of the Incarnation and the intimate relationship it has forged between the human and divine. Christian prayer is effective only because it is done through, with, and in Christ, the one and only mediator between God and humanity. Christian prayer is fundamentally "Christological." This means that without the incarnate Christ, there would be no possibility of communion with God.

Incarnation has important implications
for the life of discipleship.

Jesus asks us to follow in his footsteps by walking the path
of selfless love. The divine self-emptying that took place in the
Incarnation embodies the essence of such love. By placing his
love for humanity before all else, God humbled himself to such
an extent that he was willing to enter his own creation and take
on the limitations of human existence. In doing so, he set the
course for everything else that would happen in the life of this
newborn child. Jesus' whole life, mission, and paschal mystery
are summed up and beautifully contained in the *kenosis*, the divine self-emptying that has taken place in the mystery of the Incarnation. We follow in his footsteps by embodying this selfless love in our own lives. The Word of God is being born within our hearts when we spread the Good News of God's unconditional love for humanity to all the corners of the earth.

The Incarnation is the basic premise from which the life of discipleship flows.

Conclusion

The mystery of the Incarnation is God's response to a world gone awry. It speaks of God's unconditional love for humanity and his decision to renew it from within in a new and highly imaginative way. Rather than viewing the present world as intrinsically evil, an illusion, or a prison entrapping souls in an endless cycle of death and rebirth, the mystery of the Incarnation affirms that God, who created the world, is the Lord of history. He entered our world to save it and gave us a concrete expression of his love. This mystery set the stage for the world's redemption and the new creation. Without it, we wouldn't have known the extent of God's love for us and what he was willing to endure to save us.

This mystery lies at the heart of the Good News. It is no mistake that three of the four Gospels in the New Testament have some version of the mystery of Jesus' origins (Matthew 1—2:23, Luke 1—2:52, John 1:1-18). The differences in these accounts point to the mystery's elusive character and the inability of any human attempt to fully convey its meaning. Even the Gospel of Mark, which opens with an account of John the Baptist's baptism of Jesus (Mark 1:1-13), recognizes the latter's divine nature and gives him the enigmatic title of "Son of God."

In the end, the mystery of the Incarnation is not an obscure doctrine with no relevance to our lives today. It is the basic premise from which a life of discipleship flows. From it, we understand that the entrance of God's Word into the world is happening right now, spiritually, in the heart of his mystical body, the Church, and in the hearts of each of us. For this reason, we are called to continue Christ's universal mission of mirroring God's love to the world, serving those in need, and announcing the coming of his kingdom.

Deepening Our Awareness

- How does your image of God affect your belief in the mystery of the Incarnation?

- Was the Incarnation necessary for humanity's redemption? Was it necessary for the world's re-creation?

- Why did God choose this way to redeem humanity? Could it have occurred another way?

- What does the Incarnation mean for the life of the Church? What does it mean for your life?

- How does the mystery of the Incarnation affect your belief system? Is it an important part of your faith or something you've normally overlooked?

- Do you believe God's Word is being born within your heart? How do you relate this spiritual birth to the mystery of the Incarnation?

A Disciple's Prayer

Lord, it is difficult for me to comprehend the extent of your love for the world. It was love that moved you to send your Son to heal my wounds and to elevate me to new heights. It was love that made you become human so that I might become divine. You came to me in the most unexpected of ways: not as a king in royal splendor but as a child wrapped in swaddling clothes lying in a manger. From birth to death, you experienced human life to the fullest and were like me in all things but sin. Lord, thank you for entering the world in this way. Thank you for becoming one of us and for experiencing all that it means to be human. Help me to welcome you as you are being born this day in the cave of my heart. Shape my heart, Lord. Create it anew. Help me to empty myself and follow the path you have set out for me. Amen.

Chapter Three

He Gave of Himself Completely

At noon darkness came over the whole land until three in the afternoon. And at three o'clock Jesus cried out in a loud voice, *"Eloi, Eloi, lema sabachthani?"* which is translated, "My God, my God, why have you forsaken me?" Some of the bystanders who heard it said, "Look, he is calling Elijah." One of them ran, soaked a sponge with wine, put it on a reed, and gave it to him to drink, saying, "Wait, let us see if Elijah comes to take him down." Jesus gave a loud cry and breathed his last. The veil of the sanctuary was torn in two from top to bottom. When the centurion who stood facing him saw how he breathed his last he said, "Truly this man was the Son of God!"

Mark 15:33–39

Key Themes

- As a prophet, Jesus boldly proclaims that God's kingdom is both to come and somehow already in our midst.

- As high priest of the New Covenant, Jesus gave himself up to death and opened the way to salvation.

- As king, Jesus established a new universal order governed by the love of enemies, the practice of the beatitudes, and the rule of selfless giving.

God's love for humanity was so great that he not only came into our world but gave of himself completely, dying for us. This expression of love is best summarized by St. Paul's famous words in Philippians: "he humbled himself, becoming obedient to death, even death on a cross" (Philippians 2:8). This sentence describes the extent of Christ's love for us and the divine character of his humility. Christ's *kenosis* reveals the meaning of his divine love and provides us with a fitting model of Christian service. Christ gave of himself completely in his birth, in his ministry, in his obedient acceptance of death on a cross. This is why the meaning of Christ and all Christian existence can be characterized through the role of the servant. In one sense, Jesus spent all of his life on earth building community: his gathering of disciples, his openness to sinners, his healing of lepers and outcasts, his challenge to the religious authorities of his day. All these things represent an attempt to fashion a new Israel from the old, one that would eventually extend its embrace to all of humanity. Jesus accepted the cross because of his conviction that this act would herald in a new age for the community of Israel.

Christ's Public Ministry

By studying the narrative of Jesus' life and public ministry we can better understand what he sought to accomplish and why it was worth giving up everything. Jesus' mission defined his life. He was like us in all things, yet he never fell short of carrying out the will of his Father in heaven. We are encouraged to walk in his way and are reminded that to do so means living in humble recognition of our limitations and in eager anticipation of the coming of the kingdom.[14]

Jesus' identity as the Son of God provides us with an important key to understanding his life and mission. He lived and acted with a purpose hidden in the depths of his intimate relationship with the Father. This relationship influenced his conscious thoughts and unconscious desires and lay behind his hidden life in Nazareth, his public ministry in Galilee and Judea, and his sacrifice on Golgotha. It also lay behind those moments of solitude with God he sought in desert wastelands and on lonely mountaintops, as well as in those dramatic, symbolic actions of baptism and table fellowship that marked the beginning and end of his public ministry. Everything Jesus did, from his challenging teachings to his miraculous cures, pointed to the Father and to the coming of God's reign.

All Christian existence can be characterized through the role of the servant.

By entering our world, living among us, giving himself to us, and dying for us, he made his relationship with the Father available to us. As a result, he no longer calls us slaves, but friends (John 15:15). On Easter morning, he rose as the new

Adam, the firstborn of the new creation, and we rose with him as members of his body and the Father's adopted sons and daughters (Romans 8:14–17). Even the prodigals among us receive the same loving and compassionate attention (Luke 15:11–32). For Jesus, the reign of God was all about establishing a new order of relationships based on God's unending love for humanity. Because he relates to us as his brothers and sisters we are called to do the same in our relationships with him and one another.[15]

In his life and ministry, Jesus fostered an ever-growing circle of kingdom-oriented relationships. What began at Bethlehem with his Incarnation was nurtured at Nazareth in his immediate family life with Joseph and among many of his kin, neighbors, and fellow villagers. These relationships from Jesus' so-called hidden life were eventually extended to those in his public ministry in Galilee and Judea to include all people, especially the poor and oppressed, outcasts, and those in need of physical and spiritual healing. After his passion, death, and resurrection, they were offered to everyone who ever lived and ever would live.

Jesus' relationship with the Father ties all these facets of his life together:

- What once existed only between the Father and his only begotten Son was freely given to humanity through Mary's grace-filled *fiat* and had repercussions for Jesus' hidden life and public ministry.

- What was once hidden was made public and universal.

- What was deep in the depths of the Father's love took flesh in the womb of Mary, became visible at Bethlehem, grew and matured in Nazareth, became public in Jesus' ministry, and universal in the paschal mystery.

Death by Crucifixion

Hardly anyone disputes the historical claim made in the Apostles' Creed that Jesus "suffered under Pontius Pilate, was crucified, died and was buried."[16] While the Gospel accounts differ in their details, they are remarkably clear on who killed the carpenter of Nazareth and who gave the direct order. This indisputable fact roots the Christian faith in history and gave early believers an important historical context for their ongoing reflection on the meaning of the Christ event.

Little is known about the place of Jesus' death. In Roman times, Calvary—or *Golgotha* as it is known in Aramaic—was used as a place of execution. No one knows precisely why it was called "the place of the skull." Christians of later centuries envisioned the skulls of unburied criminals lying around, visible to the eye. Others saw a skull-like shape in the physical contours of the hill. Of all the interpretations, the one that has the greatest impact on the Christian imagination claims that the skull of Adam lies buried there. According to this early Christian tradition, the cross of Christ was planted in the dust of Adam's flesh.

Regardless of how it is interpreted, the symbol of Golgotha as the place where Christ, the new Adam, confronted the darkness of humanity's past lives on in the imagination of the Christian faithful and is crucial to understanding and growing in our faith. Meditating on the passion is essential for maintaining a healthy spiritual life. Only by plumbing the depths of Christ's suffering will we ever grasp the meaning of our own human suffering and be able to move beyond it. We must receive the cross of Golgotha before we can participate in the urgency and joy of the empty tomb. The glory of Easter comes with a price.

Jesus' death was horrible and excruciatingly painful. The Romans used crucifixion to break the criminal down physically, emotionally, socially, and even spiritually. In Jesus' day, it was a brutal reminder of Roman occupation and domination. Stoning—the typical Jewish form of capital punishment— was, compared to crucifixion, relatively quick and painless. The Romans used fear to dominate nations. Crucifixion was a principal tool in their repertoire, one that many feared and few had the courage to face, let alone endure. What happened to Jesus on Good Friday was exceedingly brutal but nothing unusual by Roman standards. So why would Jesus embrace such horrific suffering, and what does it mean for us?

For centuries, Christians have asked themselves this and similar questions as they reflected upon the meaning of Jesus' passion and death. Although the answers vary in details, they almost always agree that he suffered and died to free us from our sins and to manifest God's unending love for us.

Someone once said, "There is a cross in God before the wood is seen upon Calvary."[17] Some find such words enigmatic and difficult to accept. Suffering, after all, is not a goal to strive for but something to put up with and overcome. How could suffering exist in the heart of God? To say that there is a cross in God even before Jesus' death on Calvary takes the Christian understanding of God one step further and offers a profound insight into the mystery of God's inner life. "No one has greater love than this, to lay down one's life for one's friends" (John 15:13). Jesus' crucifixion was a defining moment of his life. It says something about who he was and what he stood for; it should also tell us something about his relationship to the Father. If God's nature is defined by love then the cross, as the symbol of love par excellence, *had* to be in God before the wood was seen on Calvary. The difficulty comes when we recognize that that same cross is also a symbol of deep human anguish.

Can love and suffering be separated? That depends. There are different types of love, just as there are different types of suffering. God's love is called charity (*caritas* in Latin; *agape* in Greek) and is associated with the selfless giving of oneself to another. In its human embodiment, Thomas Aquinas says it "makes man a friend of God."[18] In its most general sense, "suffering" means enduring some kind of pain, whether it is physical, psychological, spiritual, or even social. If divine love can have a human embodiment, perhaps human suffering (or something like it) can also exist in God. After all, the human person is created in God's own image and likeness.

So why would Jesus embrace such horrific suffering, and what does it mean for us?

For us to love as God loves doesn't mean we must endure some kind of pain for someone at all costs. What it does imply is that we should be *willing* to do so if the need arises. God does not want to suffer; he suffers because he refuses to abandon us. "My Father, if it is not possible that this cup pass without my drinking it, your will be done!" (Matthew 26:42). There was agony in God *before* the Son's agony in the Garden and on the cross—and even *after*.

Jesus' death on the cross says something about his relationship with the Father and about the nature of God. God has a heart—and it can be broken. He was willing to become one of us and die for us to mend our hearts and make us whole. Our God is a God of compassion. He suffers not only *for* us but *with* us. Was there a cross in God before the wood was seen on Calvary? There certainly was. If not, Calvary would never have happened, and we would never have known the joy of God's friendship.

Through Jesus' death, the cross—that symbol of Roman brutality and domination—was transformed into the distinctive symbol of a new religion, and his testimony from it marks the beginning of this important change. A verse from the prophet Isaiah says it best: "They shall beat their swords into plowshares and their spears into pruning hooks" (Isaiah 2:4). Jesus teaches us how to do this. He encountered the cross and embraced it. He responded to the violence of the Roman Empire with the silent message of a different kind of kingdom. Through his death, he took an instrument of execution and turned it into a lasting sign of hope and comfort for countless millions.

Real-World View: A Story of Faith

This is my commandment: love one another
as I love you.

John 15:12

In the months that followed, Jim and Dorothy spent more and more time together. On Dorothy's first day back to work, Jim made light of the incident at the Christmas party, making it easier for her to face her coworkers. The two started taking their coffee breaks together and often found themselves sitting at the same table for lunch in the company cafeteria. They talked about all sorts of things, from their favorite foods, to what they watched the night before on TV, to their favorite pastimes, and countless other little details. Sometimes the conversations became more personal, even intimate.

Jim told Dorothy about the counseling sessions he was attending, and she expressed some interest in seeking professional help for herself. She even decided to take the plunge and started attending AA meetings. She asked Jim if he would be her sponsor and he agreed. He was a constant support to her as she struggled to take a thorough inventory of her life and deal with the issues she had been unwilling to face for so many years. It took time, but slowly and surely, she was taking control of her life.

She leaned on Jim. She trusted him. He was the first person she told about the abortion of many years ago. She broke down in tears when she told him. She felt so ashamed and couldn't look him in the eyes. But Jim simply put his arms around her, gave her a big hug, and told her that it was time to let go of the burden she had buried deep in her heart. He also encouraged her to speak to her lost child, even ask forgiveness for what she had done.

This opened something new in Dorothy. She had never thought about speaking with her child before. She decided to give her child a face, even a name. She called her child Faith because that was something lacking in her own life. She wondered what she could say to her daughter, and Jim told her to simply try to express the sorrow in her heart.

Dorothy followed Jim's advice. Picturing her daughter in her mind, using her name, Dorothy spoke to her and asked her for forgiveness, beginning a process of healing. Talking to her child also fanned in her heart the burning embers of faith. In time, she found herself talking not only to Faith but also to God. She even found herself going to her local church on a late Saturday afternoon for confession. When she left the church that evening, she felt a peace in her heart that she hadn't felt since before the abortion.

She looked back on the past months and realized that she owed so much to Jim and his constant support.

Reflect

• How does Jim's love and attention for Dorothy reflect God's love?

• What is remarkable about it?

• In what way is the power of God's love acting through Jim? Are we capable of loving in this way without God's help?

Taking a Deeper Look: Jesus' Death

Jesus' public ministry and sacrificial death have implications for what we believe and for the practice of our faith. By looking more closely at his life of selfless giving that culminated in his sacrificial death, we can gain important insights into what he asks of us.

Jesus emptied himself throughout his life.

The entire sweep of his earthly life—from his birth in Bethlehem, to his hidden life in Nazareth, to his public ministry in Galilee and Judea, to his death on Golgotha and beyond— is an expression of God's unconditional and selfless love for humanity, especially for the poor, the oppressed, and those marginalized by society. Rather than categorizing Jesus' life into separate periods (for instance, birth, hidden life, public ministry, paschal mystery), it is much more helpful to see them as part of an unfolding plan. God's redemptive action doesn't take place in a single event such as Jesus' death on the cross but in the entire life, death, and resurrection of Jesus Christ, continuing through his mission, the Church.

Jesus' whole life was redemptive.

Jesus' public ministry, teachings, expulsion of demons, healings, and miracles must be seen as an integral part of his redemptive mission, one that not only anticipates the culminating events of Good Friday and Easter morning but also continues throughout history in the Church. Jesus' paschal mystery is not an isolated event but a pivotal hinge that makes it possible for his earthly proclamation of the kingdom to be projected onto a larger scale. Christ is present to his new creation through the influence of his Spirit, who animates and enlivens his followers.

The intimate relationship between Jesus' public ministry and his paschal mystery is reflected in his institution of the sacraments.

Jesus begins his public ministry after his baptism by John in the Jordan (Mark 1:9–11, Matthew 3:13–17, Luke 3:21–22) and ends it the night before his death by celebrating the Last Supper with his closest disciples (Mark 14:22–26, Matthew 26:26–30, Luke 22:15–20). This sacramental context ties Jesus' teaching and healing in an intimate way to his passion, death, and resurrection. The sacraments themselves immerse us in Christ's paschal mystery and are now the ordinary means by which we gain access to Christ's saving mysteries today.

Jesus' death at the hands of the Romans represents the culmination of Jesus' divine self-emptying.

This sort of public execution represented failure in the eyes of men and brought shame to the individual and those connected with him. At the time of his death, Jesus was deemed by nearly everyone as a complete and utter failure. The hope he had inspired in his followers had dissipated. He had been left alone, suspended in the air, and left to bleed profusely and eventually suffocate to death. In this moment of darkness, he still found within himself the capacity to trust in the power of the Father's love. Jesus' death encourages us to look at our own failures and face the shameful and humiliating moments of our lives with courage and quiet trust in God's promises.

Jesus' death on the cross is perfect selfless giving.

Early on in his public ministry, he taught his disciples to love their enemies and pray for their persecutors (Matthew 5:44). As he hangs from the cross, he demonstrates that he lived what he taught, even in death. When he asks his Father to forgive his tormentors, he does so from a heart that will be pierced by the lance of the ones he is forgiving. By asking his Father to forgive, he teaches us that to hurt another person deliberately and unjustly is a sin against God. As a result, the person who hurts another in this way ultimately hurts himself or herself in the process. This self-inflicted wound is what Jesus sees when he looks down from the cross and gazes upon his tormentors. Moved with compassion for them, he turns to his Father in heaven and intercedes on their behalf. He does the same for us. Through his death, he takes our sins upon himself and pleads our cause.

Jesus' sense of abandonment embraced every dimension of his being.

In this tortured state, Jesus entered the depths of our broken humanity and brought it back to wholeness. He did so by confronting the powers of darkness with the power of love. His death on the cross would ultimately show that love was stronger than death and formed the underlying fabric of reality. At this critical juncture of his life, he had one fundamental choice before him: to despair of life and of all he hoped for or to trust that even though the Father seemed distant and far away, his love would be there for him. Jesus chose the latter and never doubted his decision. Aided by his Spirit, he invites us to follow suit.

Jesus represents both God's gift to humanity and humanity's gift to God.

Jesus is the Redeemer, God's gift to humanity. "To redeem" means to recover or buy back. Death on the cross was the price God paid to release us from the stranglehold that sin and death had over us. There is, however, another side to the story. Because Jesus was not only divine but also fully human, his death on the cross also represents our gift to God. Jesus was like us in all things but sin. By entering our world and becoming one of us, he was able to intercede for us on our behalf. Jesus stood in our place and continues to intercede for us to this day. Through his innocent death, he offered to God what we could not: a single act of boundless love. In doing so, he made our fellowship with God possible.

In his dying moments, Jesus gave himself to the Father and to us.

Jesus' passion and death stand as a model of courage for his followers to imitate. Down through the centuries, generations of Christians would look to the cross and see in the bloodied corpus hanging from it both a challenge and a call. The challenge is to dare to trust in him as he trusted in the Father. The call is to pick up our own crosses and follow in his steps. Jesus' cross is always challenging and calling us. No matter where we are, it stands as a reminder of someone who gave all of his life in order that we might live. His challenge and his call ask us to do the same for others.

Jesus' suffering and death continue in the members of his body.

Because we have been immersed in Jesus' paschal mystery, we participate in his suffering and death. We will be crucified on the crosses we shoulder for him. We will suffer innocently from wounds inflicted upon our bodies and souls. The crucifix serves as a reminder of what Jesus went through for us and of what he is asking us to go through for him

Because of Jesus' suffering and death, our own suffering and death take on new meaning.

and for others. We, too, must face our suffering and eventual death with expectant apprehension, enduring patience, and steadfast perseverance. Our suffering will serve as a window to eternity, opening us up to the intimate life of the Godhead. Because of Jesus' suffering and death, our own suffering and death take on new meaning.

When Jesus commends his spirit to the Father, he offers with it the spirit of all humanity (Luke 23:46).

In his final act of earthly freedom, Jesus entrusts his human spirit to the Father's care. In this final act, Jesus acts as the true mediator between God and humanity. In his last words, he prays the prayer we longed to pray but could not. He takes us with him as he faces death and places us with him in the Father's care. We face death together and will overcome it together. Jesus has identified himself so closely with humanity that his story has become our story, and our story, his.

Conclusion

Jesus identified with us so closely that he bore the full weight of our human sinfulness. His innocence replaced our guilt, and his nearness to the Father eliminated the distance separating us from the divine. Jesus entered our world not to condemn it but to save it (John 3:17). He did so by giving himself to us completely and by embracing death on our behalf so that our destiny could be inexorably bound with his. His destiny was to live and die by the power of love, a force he unleashed on the world through his suffering and death on the cross.

Through the wood of the cross, Jesus defeated the power of death with the power of love. Although death embraced Jesus, it could not subdue him, for he had overcome his fear of death and commended his spirit to his Father's care. That care is our hope and the cause of our salvation. It binds up our wounds and heals our hearts. It brings us back to health and leads us to new life. It shows us the way to the kingdom and enables us, with Jesus, to share in the riches of the Father's glory. Just as Moses raised the serpent on a pole to heal all who cast their eyes upon it from the venom within them (Numbers 21: 4–9), so was Jesus lifted up on the wood of the cross to bring eternal life to all who look to him in faith (John 3:14–15). Wandering through the desert with venom in our veins is an apt description of the human situation. Moses

Because of Jesus' death on the cross, the deadly venom flowing through our veins has been extracted, the antidote generously applied.

gained healing for his people by interceding to God on their behalf. Jesus does the same and gains healing for us not from a single encounter but from death itself. Because of Jesus' death on the cross, the deadly venom flowing through our veins has been extracted, the antidote generously applied.

The suffering of the cross stems from the call to discipleship. When we shoulder our cross and follow the way of the Lord Jesus, the meaning of Golgotha takes on deeper significance. We are not just children of Adam. We are also friends and followers of Christ. We, who carry the dust of Adam in our blood, also carry the cross of Christ in our hearts. When Adam ate from the tree of Eden, it caused division within himself, in his relationship with Eve, in his stewardship of the earth, and in his fellowship with God. The tree of Golgotha promises to heal these deep wounds in the spirit and soul of humanity. The cross of Golgotha will not force its way into the soil of a hardened heart. We must allow it to penetrate our hearts.

Deepening Our Awareness

- How would you explain the reason for Jesus' sacrificial self-emptying? Is it a necessity or a free expression of will? Could it be both?

- Does this process of self-emptying last throughout Jesus' entire earthly life or just a few intense moments of it? How is it manifested in each stage of Jesus' life on earth (birth, hidden life, ministry, death, and resurrection)?

- Is Jesus' emptying of self an action of his divinity or his humanity? How does it relate to each of his roles (servant, prophet, Savior)?

- What is the relationship between Jesus' emptying of self and his love for humanity? What does it say about his love for the world?

- To what extent does the Church share in his self-emptying?

- To what extent is this self-emptying present in the lives of his followers? What does it mean for your life of discipleship?

- In what ways have you given of yourself to others? Do you give completely or do you tend to hold something back?

A Disciple's Prayer

Lord, your passion and death are a testament to your deep love for me. Your death was not necessary. You could have redeemed the world through a simple word or gesture, through a single tear or drop of blood. Yet, you chose to show us the depths of your love. You told your disciples there was no greater love than to lay down your life for your friends—and that's what you did. You suffered the most horrible death imaginable, death on a Roman cross. It is difficult for me to look at you upon the cross. You suffered and died for me! You did this to root out evil in the heart of humanity and in my own heart. There is nothing I could ever do to repay you for what you did and are doing for me at this moment. Because of you, I know what it means to be loved. Because of you, I have found that I also can love. Because of you, I do not fear suffering and am not afraid of death. Thank you for dying for me, Lord. As I look to the cross, I ask you to help me take up my own cross daily and shoulder it bravely. Help me to unite my sufferings with yours. Amen.

Chapter Four

He Became Our Nourishment

> For I received from the Lord what I also handed on to you, that the Lord Jesus, on the night he was handed over, took bread, and, after he had given thanks, broke it and said, "This is my body that is for you. Do this in remembrance of me." In the same way also the cup, after supper, saying, "This cup is the new covenant in my blood. Do this, as often as you drink it, in remembrance of me." For as often as you eat this bread and drink the cup, you proclaim the death of the Lord until he comes.
>
> *1 Corinthians 11:23–26*

Key Themes

- The Eucharist provides spiritual strength and nourishment.

- As a foretaste of the heavenly banquet, the Eucharist preserves the hope that the reign of God will one day be fully realized.

- Because Christ's death extends beyond the bounds of time, it may now be invoked at any point along the continuum of history.

- The celebration of the Eucharist is a sacramental realization of the veritable culmination of the whole of salvation history.

God not only entered our world and gave of himself completely, but he also became our food and nourishment. In his final meal on earth, Jesus performed a prophetic action revealing the heart of his messianic identity. Gathering his closest disciples around him, Jesus of Nazareth offered bread and wine as the symbols of the New Covenant soon to be ratified by his blood. This sacrament represents both a foreshadowing and a continuation of his sacrificial death. He has given of himself completely, to the point of dying and beyond, to become nourishment for us. It is in this manner that Jesus offered his Body and Blood as food for a redeemed humanity. Whenever we celebrate the Eucharist, we remember Christ's death and anticipate his future coming with joy. The Eucharist extends to all of humanity and applies throughout all time the effects of Christ's passion, death, and resurrection.

When we receive the Eucharist, Jesus' story becomes our own and ours his. From it we receive:

- insight into our call and sustenance for our journey,
- light for guidance and the grace to endure,
- the Good News,
- apostolic witness, and
- the New Testament and our Christian community.

The Eucharist is mystery. It is divine love. It is eternal life. It is manna from heaven. It is living bread. It is real food and real drink. It is all at once what Christ is and what we can and will become.

A Prophetic Action

Jesus' words of blessing on the evening before his death make little sense unless they are understood as a prophetic action that symbolically presents the establishment of a New Covenant between God and humanity. The bread and wine he shares with his disciples signifies the sacrifice of his body and blood to be given up and poured out for the sake of many. By placing his passion and death in the context of his last Passover meal, Jesus provides his followers with a concrete way of remembering him that exists in continuity with the tradition of their ancestors and raises their awareness of a new, definitive action of God in their lives.

Through this action Jesus communicates the truth of his redemptive mission. He stands in marked continuity with the Hebrew tradition. The prophetic use of concrete signs and actions to convey the message of Yahweh to his people appears frequently in the Old Testament. Including:

- Hosea's marriage to the faithless Gomer (Hosea 1:2–9),

- Jeremiah's symbols of the loincloth (Jeremiah 13:1–11),

- the shattered wine jugs (Jeremiah 13:12–14), and

- Ezekiel's making of bread from a single pot of wheat, barley, beans, lentils, millet, and spelt (Ezekiel 4:9).

What is so often forgotten when interpreting these signs and actions is that they are authentic utterances of the word of God that actually bring into effect what they symbolize. When understood in this sense, Jesus' breaking of the bread and drinking from the cup in the company of his disciples brings the event of Calvary into their midst. Before his death, Jesus brings into our midst the redeeming effects of that first Good Friday in the bread and wine he eats and drinks with his disciples. These effects culminate in his Easter rising and are already anticipated in his ministry of teaching and healing.

The Last Supper embodies Jesus' desire to be remembered for everything his life encompassed. Through the action of breaking bread and drinking from the cup, he links this sacrament of the New Covenant with all the events preceding and following his death. The Gospels emphasize this desire in clear ways. In Matthew, Mark, and Luke, symbolic actions both introduce and conclude his public ministry:

- It begins with his baptism by John in the Jordan (Matthew 3:13–17, Mark 1:9–11, Luke 3:21–22).

- It ends with the first Eucharist (Matthew 26:26–30, Mark 14:22–26, Luke 22:19–20).

In the Gospel of John, which does not include Jesus' baptism or the actual words of institution, the account of his public ministry contains many allusions to the eucharistic banquet:

- changing the water into wine at Cana (2:1–12),
- the miracle of the loaves (6:1–15),
- his discourse at Capernaum (6:22–66, especially verses 32–58),
- the discourse on the vine and the branches (15:1–17), and
- the meal of bread and fish (21:9–14).

The implication is clear. While Jesus' words of institution link the Last Supper with the events of his passion and death, the evangelists—writing under the inspiration of the Holy Spirit—also associate it with the events of his public ministry. The authors of the Gospels of Matthew, Mark, and Luke achieve this connection by using the symbolic actions of the Lord's baptism and Last Supper as a means of defining the limits of his public ministry. The author of the Gospel of John does so by filling the account of Jesus' ministry of teaching and healing with numerous eucharistic undertones. The Eucharist is connected as much to the life and public ministry as it is to the death of Jesus. Both point to what stands out as the culminating event of his life and death: his resurrection on Easter.

In the Breaking of the Bread

Rooted in this long tradition of Hebrew prophetic utterance, Jesus' institution of the Eucharist takes place in the context of a sacred meal celebrated with his disciples. His disciples and the communities they established soon come to recognize that the thanksgiving they gave to God in their breaking of the bread and drinking from the cup did indeed involve a foretaste of the heavenly banquet, the continuing presence of the risen Lord in their midst, and the sacrificial reality of Christ's redemptive death.

The Eucharist as Banquet. The relationship of the Eucharist to the fellowship of a sacred meal seems obvious. Like its Jewish counterpart Passover, the celebration of the Eucharist commemorates the great saving acts of God on behalf of his people. Its purpose is to bind Christians together through a telling of Jesus' passion, death, and resurrection and then through the ritualistic sharing in the bread and cup, which Christ likened to the eating of his own body and blood. The Eucharist serves as a focus of identity for us as Christian people. By remembering the stories and performing the actions that Jesus asked us to do in his memory, we find ourselves drawing closer to one another and building community. When considered as a meal or banquet, the Eucharist receives almost universal acclaim: Christians of all denominations affirm the importance of the great spiritual strength they receive from their gathering in fellowship around the table of the Lord.

The Eucharist as Presence. The Gospel story of the road to Emmaus (Luke 24:13–35) affirms that the risen Christ was present to his followers in numerous ways: in their walk along the road (verse 15), in their discussion of recent events (verses 16–24), in the explanation of the Scriptures (verses 25–27), and, most especially, "in the breaking of the bread" (verses 30–31). The latter involves not only the presence of Jesus but also knowledge of this presence on the part of his disciples. This recognition comes in the eucharistic action of the *breaking* of the bread and signifies Christ's dynamic personal presence to the community of believers during their celebration of the great commemorative action of his redemptive love. In their remembering, believers recognize the person of Christ in the midst of this sacramental action.

Christ is present in similar ways during today's eucharistic celebrations:

- in the gathering and going forth of the community,
- in the reading of the Scriptures,
- in the accompanying homiletic reflection, and
- the breaking of the bread.

Most especially, Christ is present during the eucharistic celebration, when the bread and wine are actually changed into the true Body and Blood of the risen Lord and given to those gathered for their spiritual nourishment.

The Eucharist as Sacrifice. When discussing the way in which the eucharistic celebration participates in the sacrifice on Calvary, the tendency in the Catholic tradition has been to emphasize the eternal aspect of Christ's redemptive offering and its ability to enter the realm of history at any moment in time and place. The strength of such an expression is that it joins the action of the Mass to Christ's sacrifice on the cross without turning the Mass into a historical reenactment of Calvary.

Christ's redemptive offering on Calvary is made present in the Mass not only through its reality as an event but also in the mysterious events that come before and after it. This means that the redemptive truth of Christ's bloody death presupposes both his becoming a man and his being raised on Easter. In this respect, Christ's redemption of humanity encompasses his entire life and is made present in the Church's celebration of the Eucharist. In the dramatic action of every Mass, Christ's becoming man, dying on the cross, and rising from the dead engage all who partake of the bread that is his Body and the wine that is his Blood. It is in receiving the Body and Blood of the risen Lord that we receive the effects of his redemptive action and are able to carry on his ministry of healing and teaching.

Real-World View: A Story of Faith

> While they were eating, Jesus took a loaf of bread, and
> after blessing it he broke it, gave it to his disciples, and
> said, "Take, eat; this is my body."
>
> *Matthew 26:26*

In time, Dorothy and Jim became more than just friends and started dating regularly. One of their favorite dates was to catch a movie on Saturday evening and then have a meal together at their favorite downtown restaurant. It became a regular ritual in their lives and something they looked forward to at the end of each week. It never really mattered what they talked about during these Saturday dinners. There were even long periods of time when they said nothing at all, just sitting in silence and resting in each other's presence.

Sharing this meal together helped them appreciate the love they shared. During those times, they also sensed they were sharing more than a meal. They could sense they were sharing their lives with each other. Jim was nourishing Dorothy and Dorothy, Jim. They shared their innermost thoughts with each other and eventually started talking about getting married. This was an important step in their lives, and they wanted to do it right. They knew life was short.

Dorothy had started going back to church on a regular basis, had rediscovered her faith in God, and buried her feelings of pain, guilt, and loss. She shared her faith with Jim, and he found his own spirituality sharpened through her sharing. They started attending Sunday Mass and sharing that experience together, too. They felt that God had drawn them together, and they wanted to share their love with him.

Attending Sunday Mass together became another important ritual in their lives, something they looked forward to each week as well. They looked forward to receiving the Eucharist each week. They felt that it brought them closer both to God and one another. It made them feel as though they belonged to a community, to something larger than themselves. In a special way, Dorothy felt that it also brought her closer to her child, Faith, as well.

Reflect
• •

- What do Dorothy and Jim's rituals say about the nature of their love for one another? About the nourishment they give each other?

- How does their quiet sharing of a simple meal enable them to give thanks for one another?

- In what ways have Dorothy and Jim become Eucharist for one another?

Taking a Deeper Look: The Eucharist

Words cannot exhaust the meaning of the Eucharist.

The mystery of the Eucharist exceeds our ability to explain. Although the Church must be open to new ways of understanding the mystery of Christ's action in the breaking of the bread and the drinking of the cup, it must also respect those traditional expressions that have been useful in the past. The word *transubstantiation*, for example, states that during Mass, bread and wine become the Body and Blood of the risen Lord, while retaining their appearance as bread and wine. Despite its usefulness in articulating the faith, even this venerable word does not exhaust the meaning of this mystery. However, we should still take care to incorporate the profound insights of tradition into any attempts to deepen our understanding of this mystery.

The various dimensions of the eucharistic mystery complement each other.

These dimensions provide the necessary inner logic to show how, in one simple liturgical action, the redemptive action of Christ can be made present in its cause (the Incarnation), in its reality (Calvary), and in its effects (the risen Christ). The Eucharist embodies Christ's entire paschal mystery and makes it present to those who receive it. In the breaking of the bread, the risen Christ becomes our bread and wine, just as these elements are transformed into the Body and Blood of the risen Christ. To receive this food is to participate in the sacred meal Christ shared with his apostles on the night before his death. To partake of his Body and Blood is to share in this death and to taste beforehand the delicacies of the heavenly banquet over which the risen Jesus himself, even now, presides.

The Eucharist is related to the whole of theology.

Christ is just as much the Lord of theology as he is the Lord of history, and we can see a eucharistic dimension in every theological discipline (dogmatic, moral, ascetical, mystical, sacramental, and liturgical). The Eucharist provides a way of looking at the various disciplines of theology that unifies theology with our real lives. The Eucharist lies not only at the heart of the Church's life but also at the heart of its theological reflection and in the minds and hearts of believers.

The Eucharist is both continuous with the Catholic tradition and a living mystery.

As a living mystery, the Eucharist celebrates its presence in the believing community and yearns for its final consummation at the end of time. Each generation of believers must rediscover the meaning of the sacrament for their lives. The Church assists in this process by gathering us together, retelling the Gospel stories, and celebrating the Eucharist in ways that are relevant and meaningful to our lives. This process is crucial to the ongoing presence of Christ's spirit in the Church.

The Eucharist lies not only at the heart of the Church's life but also in the hearts of believers.

We affirm the Eucharist
as "banquet," "presence," and "sacrifice."

These notions are intimately related, because they simultaneously affirm the efficacious and sacrificial nature of priestly consecration. It is in the breaking of the bread and drinking from the cup that believers through the centuries have recognized this presence of the risen Christ in their lives. Such recognition heightens our bonds of fellowship among believers as we dedicate ourselves more firmly to continuing the ministry of Christ's life of service to his people. It also emphasizes the values of table fellowship, presence to others, and service to others.

We recognize Christ's presence
most profoundly in the breaking of the bread.

The Eucharist lies at the center of the Church's life and is the point around which everything else revolves. It is during the celebration of this sacrament that the Church is at home and most itself. Deprived of this special source of strength and spiritual sustenance, we as believers as well as our Church would find it difficult to survive. The Eucharist is not an addendum to the faith, it is an embodiment of the mystery that constitutes and completes it.

The Eucharist can also nurture
an intense private devotion.

The relationship between the individual and communal dimensions of the Eucharist should be understood as inclusive and mutually affirming. As a family meal is both a social and individual experience, so is the celebration of the Eucharist. The sacred meal can be a communal celebration only if the individuals participating give their internal affirmation of its importance for their own relationship to the risen Christ. Private devotions are significant because they give us a deeper awareness of the mystery of Christ's redemptive presence and action in the eucharistic celebration.

The Eucharist draws individuals from disparate walks of life into a unified body of believers.

As the source of Christian unity, the Eucharist affirms the harmony that should exist between believers and promotes the spirituality of communion that lies at the heart of authentic Christian spirituality. To receive the Eucharist in the midst of interior division of soul (personal sin) or exterior division in the family, community, or society-at-large (social sin) denigrates the worth of Christ's sacred action and trivializes the mystery for which it stands.

The eucharistic celebration realizes the reign of God on earth.

The Eucharist orients God's people toward their final destiny. Through their reception of the Eucharist, they anticipate the full establishment of God's reign of peace and justice at the consummation of time. The sacrament gives us a glimpse of the happiness in God that we were intended to possess and points to the fullness of God's reign in our hearts, in our society, and in the world at large. The more we enter into this mystery, the deeper our awareness of the presence of God's kingdom in our midst will become and we will be better able to recognize God's presence in our hearts.

The Eucharist offers a focal point
around which we can seek to understand
the meaning of the Christian mystery.

As believers, the sacrament not only highlights some underlying themes essential to our Catholic faith but also provides a handy creedal synthesis with definite repercussions for the whole of theology. For the unbeliever, it helps explain the reason for the highly sacramental character of Catholic worship and presents some of the most basic reasons for our insistence on the close relation between the events of Holy Thursday, Good Friday, and Easter. While these levels of understanding will be different for the believer, who views the sacrament through the eyes of faith, and for the nonbeliever, who does not, they offer at least some common ground for mutual respect and understanding.

The Eucharist is not an addendum to the faith, it is an embodiment of the mystery that constitutes and completes it.

Conclusion

The sacramental extension of Christ's selfless death on the cross emphasizes the processes of self-emptying, which all who eat and drink worthily of the Lord's own Body and Blood must undergo. This process of self-effacing love highlights the participatory nature of all eucharistic worship. When we break bread together, we enter more deeply into the mystery of Christ's dying and rising. Nourished by this sacramental food, we are called to become spiritually nourishing, life-giving food for others. To celebrate the Eucharist requires a commitment to share more deeply in the life of Christ and in the life of our own believing community. As a result, each eucharistic community will always be characterized and judged by the quality of its life of service.

The Eucharist provides us with food for our journey. This food confirms us in our call to discipleship and encourages us to follow the promptings of the Spirit, who guides us along the way of conversion. It does so by strengthening the bonds between Christ and the members of his body and by gradually transforming us into the fullness of God's vision for us. The end of the Eucharist and Christ' paschal mystery is to empower us to continue a journey that will ultimately lead us to see God face to face. Hope in the *visio Dei* (beatific vision) permeates every aspect of the Christian life both as an end of our actions and as a fundamental means of achieving our human destiny.

Deepening Our Awareness

- Why is the Eucharist so central
  to the Church's life and mission?

- How would you explain its importance to someone
  who does not share your beliefs in the sacrament?

- How does the sacrament nourish you
  during your earthly pilgrimage?

- How does this sacrament point to
  the kingdom still to come?

- Why is eating and drinking the Lord's Body
  and Blood so important for the life of the believer?
  How is it a source of unity? How can it be a source
  of division?

- Why is the sacrament so important for following
  the path of Christian discipleship?

- In what sense can believers be "eucharist" for others?
  What can you do to be "eucharist" for someone
  in your life?

A Disciple's Prayer

Lord, when you celebrated your Last Supper with your disciples, you gave us food for the life of the world. It is manna from heaven, the pledge of the world's salvation, and medicine of immortality. As you emptied yourself to become a man and poured out your love for humanity on the wood of the cross, so now you enter into the simple elements of bread and wine to become nourishment that promises to transform and divinize us. In this sacrament, you immerse us in your paschal mystery, give us a foretaste of the heavenly banquet, and become present to us. You have made yourself accessible to us in a way never before imagined.

Thank you, Lord, for the food you give me in this sacrament. Thank you for becoming food and drink for me. Thank you for revealing yourself to me in the breaking of the bread. Lord, may the Eucharist transform my life so that I walk the path you have set out for me and become nourishment and strength for others. Amen.

Chapter Five

He Became Our Source of Hope

> For I handed on to you as of first importance what I also received: that Christ died for our sins in accordance with the scriptures; that he was buried; that he was raised on the third day in accordance with the scriptures; that he appeared to Cephas, then to the Twelve. After that, he appeared to more than five hundred brothers at once, most of whom are still living, though some have fallen asleep. After that he appeared to James, then to all the apostles. Last of all, as to one born abnormally, he appeared to me.
>
> *1 Corinthians 15:3–8*

Key Themes

- As an idea, the resurrection can be separated from a faith perspective, compared with other ideas about the nature of the afterlife, and rationally assessed for its strengths and weaknesses as a viable explanation of the nature of life after death.

- As a concrete faith reality, the resurrection is a supernatural event with historical consequences and is intricately bound to the faith of the primitive Christian community.

- Our attempt to understand the mystery of the resurrection must take both into account.

God not only entered our world, gave of himself completely, and nourished us but also became our source of hope. This hope is rooted in the empty tomb and the certitude of faith that rests upon the testimony of those who actually experienced the risen Lord. The proclamation of these early Christians forms the basis of what should and should not be believed. The testimony of Cephas, the Twelve, James, Paul, and all the others who have experienced the risen Lord verifies the resurrection and makes the meaning of our faith credible. We hope because others hope on account of what they saw and came to believe. If Christ were not raised, then their faith would be worthless (1 Corinthians 15:17); if their hope in Christ were limited to this life only, they would be the most pitiable of people (1 Corinthians 15:19).

The passage from 1 Corinthians at the head of this chapter is considered by many to be one of the earliest extant accounts of Christ's resurrection. In it, Paul draws an important connection between the resurrection of Christ and of the dead: "If there is no resurrection of the dead, then neither has Christ been raised" (1 Corinthians 15:13). This association has great significance for us. Christ's resurrection is not an isolated event but points to what we have in some way already experienced and hope one day to become: transformed, saved, resurrected, and wholly ourselves. Without the resurrection there is nothing to hope for. With it, there is everything. The resurrection lies at the heart of the Christian message, for Easter morning is truly the dawn of Christian hope. Without it, the whole Christian narrative unravels and loses its transforming power.

Resurrection: Source of Christian Hope

Resurrection is the word tied to a key belief common among Christians that, at some point after death, we are transformed by the power of God on every level of our human makeup and raised to a higher level of human existence in a way that always remains in continuity with our earthly life. Each of these elements is essential to the idea of resurrection as it exists in the major Christian traditions.

These characteristics also set resurrection apart from the related idea of bodily resuscitation (the raising of Lazarus, see John 11:44), as well as from other major explanations of life after death (the immortality of the soul, reincarnation, nirvana). Resurrection distinguishes itself from bodily resuscitation because it emphasizes a transformed existence in life after death; from the immortality of the soul, because it includes the bodily as well as the spiritual; from reincarnation because it insists on the fundamental continuity of life in the hereafter with a person's earthly existence; and from nirvana because individual consciousness is still a part of the resurrection.

The greatest strength of the idea of resurrection is that it safeguards our undeniable dignity on every level of our human makeup. It keeps our human nature eternally intact while saving the individual from personal extinction. Its greatest weakness is that it seems almost too good to be true, an attractive but highly unlikely possibility. Of all the ideas of life in the hereafter, resurrection is the most difficult to accept on faith alone. It stretches the limits of our imagination, challenges us to think outside the box, and encourages us to dream of the realization of our deepest hopes.

The idea of the resurrection is rooted in the Jewish tradition and continued to be taught by the Pharisees in Jesus' lifetime. The idea of resurrection developed into our current understanding after serious reflection on the nature of the Christ event, most especially in the early Christian community's interpretation of the meaning of the apostolic experience of the risen Lord. This reflection is intimately tied to the trust that community placed in the authenticity of the apostolic witness and the experience of faith upon which it rested. It is also the context within which we may speak of the resurrection not as an idea but as a reality and future hope.

What happened on that first Easter remains shrouded by the mysterious nature of the event itself and by the human responses to it by the earliest followers of Jesus. Before sharing or recording the event, they probably ran the gamut of several emotional states: depression and fear, suspicion and isolation, and incipient faith and yearning for lost expectations. That is not to say that the event has no basis outside the experience of Jesus' followers, but there is no way to determine what it is with any historical accuracy. The Easter event touches history but extends far beyond it. Probably the most important consequence of this unique eschatological/historical encounter is the faith experience of Jesus' immediate followers that provides the original impetus for the rise and spread of the earliest Christian communities. The faith of the Church rests upon the foundation of these earliest apostolic witnesses.

There is also a difference between the faith of those who witnessed the Easter event personally and those who relied on the testimony of the apostles. The proclamation of the Church rests upon the eyewitness accounts of the apostles. Their experience of faith remains different from that of the believer in the pew because they experienced a reality outside of themselves, rooted in the objective order, distinct from their own subjectivity, and identified with the person of their master, Jesus of Nazareth.

Without the unprecedented boldness and resiliency of these claims, the Christian project would have nothing distinctive in its message and might never have gotten off the ground.

These apostolic claims come from one of two possibilities: the experience of the risen Christ *with* or *without* a basis in the objective order. In other words, the experience of the apostles either corresponds to a reality outside themselves or was purely subjective. This leads to the questions:

- If their experience has its basis in the objective order, then we must ask ourselves how someone who was crucified, died, and buried could possibly rise from the dead.

- If their experience was entirely subjective, then we have to assume the apostles suffered from some kind of self-delusion, that their testimony was false, and that our entire religion is built on false witness.

The fact that neither of these possibilities can be proven highlights the underlying quality of faith in the conclusions of both believer and nonbeliever.

The charge of nonbelievers that the apostolic claims are entirely subjective with no basis in objective reality touches a sensitive point about the nature of human knowledge in general. There are those who would question the existence of objective reality and who would assert that every claim to truth is shaped (even tainted) by the perspective of human observation. For them, "objectivity" is a myth, since it is impossible to attain an entirely detached vantage point for observation. Such a claim is based on an assumption that cannot be proven in itself and that must simply be accepted at face value. To be sure, subjective experience *does* shape the way we interact with the world around us; it *does not*, however, offset the common-sense claim that the external order exists and that we have access to it through our senses. The further claim, moreover, that the apostles were suffering from some kind of self-delusion stems from the refusal to admit the possibility that the laws of nature can be broken or interfered with in any way, not even by the author of those laws himself, God, our Creator. Since someone could not possibly rise from the dead, the only alternative for the nonbeliever is to say that the apostles were somehow misled into believing something that did not actually occur. They suffered, in other words, from some kind of mass hysteria, auto-suggestion, or self-hypnosis that led them to project something they were only imagining onto the objective order.

> **The deepest longings of the human heart find fulfillment in the hope of sharing one day in Christ's glorified existence.**

More can be said about the position of the believer. If the apostolic experience of the risen Christ *does* have an objective basis in the person of Jesus, then this claim—when combined with the idea of resurrection developed above—points to an event unique to all of human history that can be verified only in part by its concrete effects (for example, a missing body). For this reason, it must be understood primarily as a supernatural event with historical consequences in time and place. In other words, since the risen Christ exists in a transformed state but in a way continuous with his earthly life, he does not lead a "historical existence" in the way we use the phrase today. Time and space no longer set the limits for his physical existence. In his resurrected state, Jesus is unique to himself.

He is the Alpha and the Omega, who gathers all of creation into the love of the Father and the joy of their Spirit. We hope to share in this resurrected life of Christ. Our faith in the risen Lord gives us hope that we will one day share in his glorified existence and stand with him in the presence of the Father. We can taste it even now and hope to experience it fully in the time to come. This hope sustains us in life as we take up our cross daily and follow Christ.

Being a disciple of Christ requires discipline and making concrete decisions about our lives.

Real-World View: A Story of Faith

So faith, hope, love remain, these three;
but the greatest of these is love.

1 Corinthians 13:13

Dorothy and Jim got married a few years after they started dating. They had a nuptial Mass and, at their request, the priest celebrated it for Dorothy's unborn child, Faith. It was a small, intimate wedding, held in the small side chapel where the parish had daily Mass. After the ceremony, they invited a few relatives and friends to their favorite restaurant, the one they always went to on Saturday evenings. They had a nice meal and various toasts and stories were exchanged.

After the cake was cut, Dorothy stood up and shared with everyone present how much Jim meant to her and how the love they shared had given her a new lease on life. She also told the story of her child, Faith, about how she had sought forgiveness from the child for what she had done and how connected she felt with her now. She also told everyone that she felt especially close to her whenever she received holy Communion. The Eucharist, she believed, was a sacrament of love, and it was only because of faith in the power of God's love that she was able to feel that forgiveness. Jim, she said, had helped her see that love was stronger than the terrible guilt that she had been carrying around for so many years.

When she finished, Jim stood up and told everyone that Dorothy was the love of his life and that he believed that God had brought them together. After all, it all began at a Christmas party, and he believed that Christ came into their lives that day in a new and vibrant way.

As they continued to grow together in their marriage Dorothy and Jim decided to add to their family and share their love. Jim suggested they adopt. Dorothy agreed, and together they came upon the idea of adopting a child whose mother had considered having an abortion. They contacted several adoption agencies and eventually were coupled with a newborn baby girl. They were so excited, so happy, and filled with so much peace.

When they were thinking about what name to give their child, they also thought about their past, before they met each other, and their future now that they were together. There was really only one name that seemed to fit. So they decided to call their new daughter Hope.

Reflect

- What do Dorothy and Jim hope for?

- How does Dorothy's love for faith lead her to hope?

- How does Dorothy and Jim's adopted child deepen this connection?

Taking a Deeper Look:
Hope and the Resurrection

The basis of Christian hope rests on the idea that the resurrection has become a reality in the risen Christ. Starting from this premise, the following points focus on some of the deepest longings of the human heart and how they find fulfillment in the hope of sharing one day in Christ's glorified existence.

Our hope in Jesus is rooted in an event that cannot be historically verified.

The resurrection of Christ exists outside of, but in relation to, the realm of historical inquiry. This claim is important for our spiritual lives since it determines whether our faith is rooted in objective reality or a purely subjective experience. As a supernatural event with effects in time, Jesus' resurrection lies beyond the realm of scientific investigation and can be affirmed only through faith in the testimony of those claiming to have actually experienced Jesus after his death. That is not to say that the apostles did not experience something outside of themselves in the external world but only that the basis for their experience cannot be verified. The only historical consequence would have been the disappearance of Jesus' body at the actual moment of his resurrection. Since the precise whereabouts of his body was a point of contention even in the initial aftermath of the Easter proclamation (Matthew 28:13), one must conclude that, although its disappearance at this time could have been verified, it was not. When confronted with the mystery of the resurrection, we must not focus merely on its scientific plausibility but on the biblical affirmation that "for God all things are possible" (Matthew 19:26). Our faith is rooted in the testimony of the apostles. If this testimony is called into question, the entire edifice of our faith collapses.

Our hope in Jesus is rooted in a belief about the reality of his resurrection and its implications for our destiny.

A detached observer may not have been able to separate the subjective experience of the apostles from the reality of the risen Christ. There may have been no way of determining whether or not they were actually experiencing anything beyond their own intensified inner awareness. The uniqueness of this experience would be expected. As a result, the faith of subsequent Christian believers is qualitatively different from that of the apostles. Not only does our faith rest on the conviction of those who claimed to have an actual experience of the risen Lord, but, in some ways, it is even a purer experience of faith: "Blessed are those who have not seen and have believed" (John 20:29). With this in mind, we are encouraged to consider the responsibility we have to foster the gift of faith with which we have been blessed and embody it in every aspect of our lives.

Our hope in Jesus is rooted in the belief that his resurrection is a part of God's plan for the world's redemption.

Since idea and reality are intimately connected in Divinity's vision of itself, the resurrection of Christ may be viewed as a providential movement on the part of the Father to bring the plan of redemption in accord with the working of the Divine Mind (the *Logos*). In this respect, Christ's resurrection is that event which, touching upon history but transcending time, initiates the ultimate return of all created things back to God. Life in the risen Christ means we are participating in this process and will ultimately share in the fruits of Christ's kingship. It also breathes new life into the significance of the principle that God became man (Incarnation) in order that humanity might become divine (share in the life of the risen Lord).

Christ's resurrection sheds light upon the development of the doctrine of the Incarnation.

The mysteries of the Incarnation and the Redemption are two sides of the same coin. If in Christ's resurrection our humanity has been divinized and lifted up into the reality of the Word through Christ's resurrection, it is easy to see how early Christians would come to believe that the Word itself had descended into the reality of human flesh and had become human. When seen in this light, the doctrines of Christ's Incarnation and resurrection form two aspects of a single salvific event which, if we were to borrow language adopted by Aquinas, represents the *re-creation* of all things *going out of* (*exitus*) and *going back to* (*reditus*) God. It is in this sense that all things are gathered or recapitulated in Christ, the new Adam (Romans 5:15). The mysteries of the Incarnation and the Redemption must be examined not in isolation but interpreted in light of each other and the underlying salvific plan they each promote.

Jesus is our source of hope not only
because he has risen from the dead but also
because he has ascended into heaven to
sit at the right hand of the Father.

His journey through life ends where it began—at the right hand of the Father. Because of the paschal mystery, Jesus' life has now become our own. We live in hope because we believe that our place is with him. This aspect of our faith brings out this ultimate, eschatological dimension of our lives. It reminds us that our decisions have consequences for our lives and that we must remain in Christ if we wish our hope to become a reality. Living in hope means affirming before every person and in every situation we face that Jesus alone is the Lord and master of life. If we call ourselves his disciples, then we cannot compromise on this fundamental premise of our faith. The interlocking of our personal narratives with Christ's is the mark of divine adoption by the Father, who by virtue of his Son's paschal mystery now looks upon us as his own sons and daughters.

The resurrection is an intricate part
of the entire process of redemption.

If Christ's going forth from the Father reaches its furthest extension in his passion and death on the cross, then his return is ushered in by the events of Easter and all that follows. When seen in this light, Christ's ascension into heaven and the sending of his Spirit at Pentecost represent a continuation of the Easter event and the culmination of Christ's redemptive activity. In the mystery of the ascension, Christ returns to his place at the right hand of the Father and brings with him our re-created and divinized humanity. At Pentecost, Christ pours out his

Spirit upon the nascent community of believers and gives birth to his mystical body, the Church. By returning to the Father and pouring his Spirit upon the community of disciples he left behind, he makes it possible for all who believe in him to join in his glorified existence. Today we view our lives as a continuation of Christ's life and ministry in time. We are the living members of Christ's body today and are called to live and act accordingly.

Our hope in Jesus is rooted in the supernatural nature of the Christ event.

Based on the testimony of its apostolic ancestors, the Church has kept alive the fervent hope that the deepest yearnings of our hearts will one day be fully realized. The transformation wrought by God in Christ promises to extend itself to all who are incorporated through faith into his body, the Church. In this respect, a sharing in the life of the risen Lord may be looked upon as the ultimate destiny of all of humanity and will be impeded only by a stubborn private or communal persistence in the life of sin. Jesus is the source of our hope because he has overcome the powers of sin and death and promises that anyone who believes in him will one day rise from the dead and share in his glorified existence. Because of Jesus we believe that sin and death have been defeated and lost their stranglehold over us. We look forward to the day when we will triumph completely over them and share in the fullness of the redemption made possible by Christ's paschal mystery.

Through his resurrection,
Jesus became a source of hope for all of humanity.

Jesus gave himself to us completely, and the empty tomb of Easter reminds us that God's love is stronger than death. Through baptism, we become members of Christ's body and are incorporated into his passion, death, and resurrection. For this reason, we also are called to be a source of hope for others. Jesus' resurrection reminds us that life does not end in death. Through faith, we join Jesus in death and hope to share in his resurrection (John 11:25). By loving others as Jesus loved us, we become a source of hope for them. Through us, they get a glimpse of God's love for them and receive an insight into the true purpose and meaning of life. Through our actions, hope becomes something concrete and tangible for them. Seeing us living in hope, they are inspired to do the same. How do we live in hope? We do so by rooting our lives in the person and message of Jesus Christ. We cherish our friendship with Jesus, look upon it as the one thing that matters in life, and seek to share our love for him with others.

Belief in the risen Christ keeps alive the hope that,
after death, our lives will not end.

Because of Christ's resurrection, we look forward to a transformed existence in the hereafter, one in continuity with our lives on earth. This hope forms the basis upon which life in the resurrection is anticipated even in the present. Through our participation in the ministry and life of the Church, we receive a foretaste of this transformed existence, especially when we partake of the sacraments around the table of the Lord. Jesus opened up the meaning of the Scriptures to his disciples when he accompanied them on the road to Emmaus, and they recognized him in the breaking of the bread (Luke 24:30). Today we seek the same when we gather in churches throughout the world to celebrate the Eucharist. We recognize Jesus in the gathering of believers, the sharing of the word, in the person of the priest, in the silence burning within our hearts, and in the breaking of the bread. The eyes of faith reveal his presence and keep alive the hope of sharing even more deeply in the fruits of his glorified existence.

Christian hope affirms that this destiny has already become a reality in the mystery of Mary's assumption.

The Blessed Mother was present at every important moment of Jesus' earthly life. She was the first to see him enter the world; she nurtured him during his hidden life in Nazareth; she accompanied him during his public ministry; she stood beneath him at the foot of the cross; she was with the community of disciples for the outpouring of the Holy Spirit at Pentecost. It was fitting that she would be the first to experience the fullness of the Redemption. Mary would be the first to have her humanity completely transformed through the fruits of Christ's Redemption so that, at this moment, her body and soul are living a glorified existence in the presence of the Father. Because of this special privilege, one that parallels her immaculate conception, Mary bears the title, "Mother of Hope." We see in her someone in whom Christ's promise of plentiful redemption has been completely fulfilled. She embodies everything we yearn for and hope to experience. She inspires us to look to her Son at all times and to hope that we also will one day share in the blessings of his glorified existence.

Although much more could be said about Christ's resurrection and origins of Christian hope, these are the main contours of the relationship. They open avenues for further inquiry and, most of all, encourage us to live in hope, with our hearts focused on the end of our earthly pilgrimage so we might have a heightened awareness of Jesus' presence in our midst as he accompanies us at every step of our journey through life, into death, and the world beyond.

Conclusion

Seen as a supernatural event with effects in time, the resurrection of Jesus of Nazareth lies beyond the scope of scientific verification and remains intimately tied to the internal, subjective event of faith to which it gave life. That is not to say that it has no grounding in the external order, only that it ultimately lies beyond the scope of controlled observation. Our hope in Jesus' resurrection comes through the eyes of faith. It rests on the eyewitness testimony of the early Christian community and their faith-filled affirmation, "He is risen!" Without it, the evangelizing power of the Gospel loses its urgency and vitality. It becomes bereft of its transforming power and is emptied of its ability to touch the deepest recesses of the human heart.

In this respect, the faith experience of those who experienced the risen Lord is different from that of those whose faith rests upon their testimony. Today we share in the hope of our own transformed existence. We bring our hearts' deepest yearning for the fullest presence of the risen Christ to the table of the Lord, where we are blessed with a glimpse of his continued presence in our eucharistic breaking of the bread. This sacrament is central to the proclamation of the Gospel message, because it puts us in direct contact with the risen and glorified Christ and is the concrete sign of hope for the in-breaking of God's kingdom and the coming of a new creation. Without it, we'd lack the nourishment and hope to sustain us on our earthly pilgrimage.

During his life on earth, Jesus possessed the fullness of hope. This awareness of his eschatological destiny was rooted not in the resurrection (which had not yet taken place) or in the testimony of his disciples (who would never have understood at the time), but in his singular mystery of his own divinity and intimate relationship to the Father. The Word provides us with hope from the deep eschatological awareness that he found in himself. The reason we hope in the resurrection of the dead is because, even before his own resurrection, it was Jesus himself who first hoped for us. That hope is kept alive today in the Church's life and mission.

Deepening Our Awareness

- In what ways is Jesus the source of our hope? What does he offer us?

- What does Jesus' resurrection tell us about our own human destiny? What promise does it hold for us?

- How is Jesus' resurrection related to the mystery of the Incarnation?

- How is it related to the mystery of his ascension, the descent of the Holy Spirit at Pentecost, and the assumption of the Blessed Virgin Mary?

- How is it related to the whole mystery of humanity's redemption?

- How has belief in Jesus' resurrection changed your outlook on the world? How has it changed your outlook on life?

- Do you believe that Jesus' resurrection and ascension make it possible for you to be an adopted son or daughter of the Father?

- How can you begin living this life today?

A Disciple's Prayer

Lord, your life did not end with your death. News of the empty tomb and your appearance to your disciples soon spread through the countryside of Judea and Galilee. People believed this Good News and many even died for it. In time, the Gospel message spread from mouth to mouth and soon became known throughout the world. The power of this message lies in what it says about the power of love. Death did not defeat you. Your love is stronger than death. Rather than the end of existence, death is a passageway to a new life, one that transforms us and carries us into the presence of our Father in heaven. Your paschal mystery reveals our future hope. You took our humanity with you so that we might one day join you in this resurrection. You gave us your Spirit to sanctify us and guide us. Lord, thank you for rising to new life. Thank you for the hope that I, too, may one day rise. Mary, Mother of Hope, deepen my trust in the promises of your Son. Help me to look both to him and to you in my time of need. Amen.

Conclusion

The Call to Discipleship

> This is my commandment: love one another as I love
> you. No one has greater love than this, to lay down
> one's life for one's friends. You are my friends if you
> do what I command you. I no longer call you slaves,
> because a slave does not know what his master is
> doing. I have called you friends, because I have told
> you everything I have heard from my Father.
>
> *John 15:12–15*

If we take a look at the story of Dorothy and Jim told throughout
this book, we can see the mystery of Jesus' own story slowly
emerging from the background and taking center stage. Like
Dorothy, we've all experienced what it means to live in a broken
world and the temptation to succumb to its empty promises.
At various times we have all felt that emptiness and the desire
to fill it with something other than God. No matter what the
circumstances are that lead us to this place, it is easy to lose
touch with God and question the meaning of our life.

117

Jesus is the God of love made flesh. He entered our broken world, gave himself to us completely, and became our nourishment and source of hope. This Gospel spirituality is clearly at work in Dorothy's life. At a relatively young age, she experienced what it meant to live in a broken world and had almost succumbed to its empty promises. Pressured into an abortion by someone she thought had loved her, she lost touch with her better self and got lost in a series of broken relationships. The ensuing emptiness she experienced within herself led her to escape her troubles by medicating herself with alcohol and prescription drugs. It also caused her to lose touch with God and, in the midst of her loneliness, question the meaning of life.

Dorothy's broken world is strangely familiar to us. Her plight is not all that different from our own. Change a few of the circumstances and her story could well be ours. Like her, we also know what it's like to have someone like Jim enter our lives (or to be the "Jim" to someone else). Whether it's through a book, a quiet walk along the shore, a homily at Mass, a coworker, friend, or romantic partner, God finds a way to enter our lives in unexpected ways. And when he does he takes our hand, pulls us out of our despair, and walks with us through our darkest moments. We can return that grace by becoming nourishment for someone else when we open up our lives and make ourselves vulnerable to others, just as Jim made himself vulnerable to Dorothy, showing her that life can get better.

As Christians, we hear the Gospel story and embrace it as our own. We believe that Christian discipleship means allowing Christ to weave the story of his life, death, and resurrection into our own lives so that we desire nothing more than to do what he did and live as he lived. Being a disciple of Christ means focusing our hearts entirely on Christ and trusting that he will show us the way to the Father. It means letting go of our self-centeredness and allowing

God to take possession of our hearts. We do this simply by inviting him into our hearts with each new day and conversing with him as a friend.

When we open our hearts to Christ in this way, we come to a deeper awareness of him and begin to see the world as he sees it. We share in the same attitudes and seek to think and act as he does. Like him, we, too, want to enter the world of those around us and give of ourselves so as to become nourishment and hope for them. Like him, we desire to serve rather than be served. Like him, we look lovingly upon others and strive to relieve them of their burdens. Like him, we want to lay down our lives for our friends. We act in this way because we are intimately tied to him as members of his mystical body. His spirit prays within us, communes with us, leads us, and empowers us to reach out to others. As a result, we receive a heightened sense of our role in the world and begin to live the Gospel on ever deeper and deeper levels of awareness.

Dorothy's life would have continued on its downward spiral had not she had the good fortune of having someone like Jim to enter her world, take her by the hand, and pull her out of the destructive emotional whirlwind. Jim not only entered her world but also walked with her and stayed with her through some of the darkest moments of her life. He gave himself to her in a way she had never before experienced so that she gradually overcame her distrust of others and actually was able to enter into an authentic, life-giving relationship. Jim became nourishment for her by opening up his own life to her and by encouraging her to seek treatment for her addictions. They started seeing more of each other and, in time, their friendship grew into something they both treasured deeply. They fell in love and knew that whatever else the future might hold, they would face it together.

Jim became a source of hope for Dorothy—and vice versa. They started dating, began going steady, and eventually got married.

Like Dorothy, we need to open ourselves to God's intervention in our lives. When we do so, we allow him to befriend us; we invite him into our lives and seek to enter into his. We converse with him from the heart and share with him our deepest thoughts and feelings. We listen to him in silence as we ponder the words of Scripture and receive him in holy Communion. In time, we experience a sense of mutual indwelling and begin to see things differently. We clothe ourselves with compassion, kindness, humility, meekness, and patience. We bear with one another and, above all, clothe ourselves with love. The peace of Christ rules in our hearts, we seek to do everything in his name, and we focus our lives on building up the family of God.

Dorothy, Jim, and their children were a family of four. Their first child was Faith, the aborted baby whom Jim had encouraged Dorothy to name and to seek forgiveness for taking her life so many years ago. Although they had never seen this child, she was very much present to them through the eyes of faith. Their second child was Hope, the baby they adopted soon after their marriage and who would be the joy of their lives for years to come. They lived for this child and did all within their power to give her a happy home and a secure future. Through it all, their marriage was sustained by the Love they shared with one another. This bond was the most precious thing in their lives, for it made their Faith come alive to them, and it led them to face their future with Hope. It also led them to bear much fruit and to nourish others in countless ways. Grateful for the love they shared, they echoed in their lives the timeless words of St. Paul, "So faith, hope, love remain, these three; but the greatest of these is love" (1 Corinthians 13:13). Dorothy and Jim experienced this love in a real and palpable way. Most of all, they knew that it was not of their own making but that it came from God.

We are called to live out our faith by building deep, loving relationships. When we do so, our faith stops being merely a long list of "do's and don'ts" and becomes instead a vibrant living out of our friendship in Christ. We understand that following Christ means loving like him and firmly believing that nothing can separate us from his own love for us. We realize that being a disciple of Christ requires discipline and making concrete decisions about our lives. We also see that it means dedicating our lives entirely to him, living out our commitments in responsible ways, and making the Gospel values the primary criteria for our actions.

This book reminds us of what it means to follow Jesus. In recounting the Christian story, it points both to the cross and the empty tomb, to the commandments and the Beatitudes, to the Law and to life in the Spirit. It tells us that discipleship is all about friendship with Christ and that its path is clearly laid out in the narrative of Jesus' paschal mystery. It reminds us that, through faith, Jesus' story has become our own and that the world's salvation is continually being played out through us, the members of his body. It tells us that we walk by faith, not by sight (2 Corinthians 5:7) and that God's kingdom is constantly breaking through the boundaries of time and space. It tells us to live not for ourselves but for others and to encourage others to do the same. It reminds us that love is stronger than death and that all things are possible with God (Matthew 19:26, Luke 1:37). It says that Jesus' disciples live and die under the standard of the cross and that the love it represents will keep them close to Christ and one day carry them into the presence of the Father. Finally, it raises questions for each of us about what it means to follow Jesus in the concrete circumstances of our daily lives:

- How are we called to respond to the broken world in which we find ourselves?

- Whose world are we called to enter?

- How can we give ourselves to them in service?

- How can we be nourishment for them?

- How can be a source of hope for them?

- Whom shall we serve, when, where, and how?

Such questions challenge us and call us to action. They demand concrete answers and heartfelt responses. They require us to take a good look at our situation and to respond in ways that reflect authentic Gospel values. They ask us to be the eyes and ears, the hands and feet, the mind and heart of Jesus in the world today. They beg us to give flesh to Jesus' message of unconditional love and to give concrete evidence that his Spirit is alive and well and at work in our hearts.

Endnotes

[1] See, for example, review of Louis Bouyer's *Introduction à la vie spirituelle* (Paris: Desclée, 1960) by Jean Daniélou, "A propos d'une introduction à la vie spirituelle," *Études* 94 (1961): 170–74 and the response by Louis Bouyer (*Ibid.,* 411–15).

[2] This fundamental principle of Gospel spirituality appeared in seminal form in Dennis J. Billy, "The Christ Kernel," *Review for Religious* 47 (1988): 594–603 and was developed in more scholarly fashion in *Idem, Evangelical Kernels: A Theological Spirituality of Religious Life* (Staten Island, NY: Alba House, 1993), 17–31. The present book is an expanded version of this basic Christian principle and seeks to make it accessible to a wider reading audience. Similarly, parts of chapters four ("He Became Our Nourishment") and five ("He Became Our Source of Hope") present, in a modified, format insights of mine that first appeared in *Idem, Evangelical Kernels*, 109–22, 135–50; *Idem*, "The Bread Kernel," *Review for Religious* 50 (1991): 749–58; *Idem*, "The Resurrection Kernel," *Review for Religious* 51 (1992): 206–16.

[3] G. K. Chesterton, *What's Wrong With the World* (London: Cassell and Co., Ltd., 1910), Part I, chap. 5.

[4] Tertullian, *Apology*, 50.12.

[5] See Second Vatican Council, **Dogmatic Constitution on the Church** *(Lumen Gentium)*, 39–42.

[6] See C. S. Lewis, *God in the Dock: Essays on Theology and Ethics*, ed. Walter Hooper (Grand Rapids, MI).

[7] See, for example, Augustine of Hippo, *The City of God*, 14.11–28.

[8] See, for example, Irenaeus of Lyons, *Against the Heresies*, 3.18.1–7; 4.34.1; 5.14.2; 5.21.2.

[9] *Catechism of the Catholic Church*, 390.

[10] See N. Max Wildier, *The Theologian and His Universe: Theology and Cosmology From the Middle Ages to the Present* (New York: The Seabury Press, 1982), 1.

[11] See the Pontifical Biblical Commission, *The Bible and Morality: Biblical Roots of Christian Conduct*, 21–38 (Vatican City: **Libreria Editrice Vaticana**, 2008), 34–56.

[12] Athanasius of Alexandria, **On the Incarnation**, 54.3.

[13] Alphonsus de Liguori, *Reflections and Affections on the Passion of Jesus Christ*, 2.8

[14] For a summary of the mysteries of Jesus' hidden and public lives, see *Catechism of the Catholic Church*, 512–70 (Vatican City: **Libreria Editrice Vaticana,** 1994), 129–46.

[15] See Second Vatican Council, *Lumen Gentium*, 2–4.

[16] From the Apostles' Creed. Cited in *the Roman Missal. The Sacramentary* (New York: Catholic Book Publishing Co., 1985), 369.

[17] Horace Bushnell, *The Vicarious Sacrifice* (1866), 35–36. Cited in Kenneth Leech, *Experiencing God: Theology as Spirituality* (San Francisco: Harpercollins, 1989), 301.

[18] Thomas Aquinas, *Summa Theologiae,* II–II, q. 172.

About the Author

Fr. Dennis J. Billy, CSsR, is a Redemptorist with advanced degrees from Harvard University, the Pontifical University of St. Thomas (Angelicum), and the Graduate Theological Foundation. He taught for more than twenty years at the Alphonsian Academy of Rome's Pontifical Lateran University and is now scholar-in-residence, professor, and holder of the John Cardinal Krol Chair of Moral Theology at St. Charles Borromeo Seminary, Overbrook, in Wynnewood, PA. He has authored numerous books and articles on various religious topics.